Critical Thinking for Social Work

Other titles in the series

To order, please contact our distributor: BEBC Distribution, Albion Close, Parkstone, Poole, BH12 3LL. Telephone: 0845 230 9000, email: **learningmatters@bebc.co.uk.** You can also find more information on each of these titles and our other learning resources at **www.learningmatters.co.uk**

Critical Thinking for Social Work

Second Edition

KEITH BROWN
LYNNE RUTTER

Series Editor: Keith Brown

LearningMatters

First published in 2006 by Learning Matters Ltd.
Second Edition published in 2008

British Library Cataloguing in Publication Data
A CIP record for this book is available from the British Library.

ISBN: 978 1 84445 157 9

Cover and text design by Code 5 Design Associates Ltd
Project Management by Deer Park Productions, Tavistock, Devon
Typeset by Pantek Arts Ltd, Maidstone, Kent
Printed and bound in Great Britain by Bell & Bain Ltd, Glasgow

Learning Matters Ltd
33 Southernhay East
Exeter EX1 1NX
Tel: 01392 215560
info@learningmatters.co.uk
www.learningmatters.co.uk

Contents

About the authors

Keith Brown
Keith holds professional qualifications in nursing, social work and teaching; and academic qualifications in nursing, social work and management. He has worked in the education and training field for over 25 years, working for three universities and three local authority social work departments. Currently he is the Director of the Centre for Post-Qualifying Social Work at Bournemouth University. In 2005 he was awarded the Linda Ammon Memorial Award, sponsored by the then Department for Education and Skills, a prize awarded to the individual making the greatest contribution to training and education in the UK.

Lynne Rutter
Lynne holds academic and professional qualifications in librarianship and education. Currently she teaches 'enabling work-based learning' and 'critical thinking' units, and offers academic support via tutorials and printed teaching materials. Lynne has an MA in academic practice and is continuing to research professional education and learning within a professional doctorate programme.

Foreword to Post-Qualifying Social Work Series

This text, *Critical Thinking for Social Work*, is one of a series of texts written by experienced social work educators and practitioners, some of whom are working the Centre for Post-Qualifying Social Work at Bournemouth University.

All the texts are written with the specific aim of supporting social workers who are studying for the Post-Qualifying Awards in their chosen field of practice/specialism. However, much of the content of each text is also valuable to students on qualifying social work programmes.

As members of the Centre for Post-Qualifying Social Work, we all work with the aim of promoting the best social work practice for the sake of all service users and their carers.

I think that you will find this text of good value in your social work career.

Keith Brown
Series Editor
Centre for Post-Qualifying Social Work

Preface to the second edition

We have been delighted with the responses to the first edition of this text and especially to hear that students and social workers have found it valuable in their studies, and in reflection of their practice.

Following all the feedback, we wanted to add to this text and update the material to produce a second edition. In particular we have added a new chapter, *Continuing learning – a critical approach*, to take account of the current emphasis on continued professional development and post-registration training and learning. Our aim is to offer some insight to support continuing learning.

We are aware that there is much to celebrate with respect to social work practice. Social workers and social work students often work with great imagination and skill with vulnerable members of society. This text is written to assist you, the practitioner, to critically reflect on and express what you do, how you do it and why you do it. We sincerely hope this text enables you to demonstrate and evidence your professional competence and capability, and enhances your learning and professional development.

Keith Brown
Lynne Rutter

Introduction

Critical thinking as a process can appear formal and academic, something far removed from everyday life where decisions have to be taken quickly in less than ideal conditions. It is therefore unhelpful to present critical thinking as a linear process or a set of techniques for everyday working conditions because we rarely have the time or opportunity to follow a strict order in our thinking. We have adopted a more holistic approach and therefore this work does not aim to be a textbook on critical thinking skills or theories. We do not aim to 'teach' critical thinking. Rather this handbook aims to act as a guide and resource, suggesting ideas from our own practice and the work of others to help you develop your own critical approaches to practice.

A recent review (Phillips and Bond, 2004) found four different conceptions for critical thinking. These are:

- as a generic skill;

- as an embedded skill;

- as a component of lifelong learning;

- for critical being.

All these notions are apparent within the circumstances and requirements of the social work degree and the post-qualifying (PQ) framework. As students you require a set of initial generic and subject-specific critical techniques to work with, but developing critical abilities within the social work arena can also enhance learning and development, and there is potential to progress your own style of critical thinking. Our concept encompasses the idea that critical thinking can be developed and embedded within existing practice abilities in order for a practitioner to deal confidently with an uncertain and ever-changing world.

Our ideas have been developed from practice experience with students over many years, and from our ongoing research and reading on the subject. In order not to interrupt the flow of ideas or detract from the informal style of this guide, we have kept referencing to a minimum. However, we fully acknowledge the ideas of others by the inclusion of all those influencing our work in the references at the end.

Structure of the handbook

The first chapter explores the many different ways this handbook can help qualifying and post-qualifying social work students as well as practitioners. In the second chapter we look at a useful conception of critical thinking as a set of 'requisite intellectual resources' (Bailin et al., 1999). These generic resources are explored further in the following chapters and are enhanced with more context-specific critical abilities, qualities and approaches appropriate for qualifying and post-qualifying practice. The handbook then provides chapters on learning, critical reflection, writing, critical practice, and lastly on continuing learning.

This handbook takes a pragmatic look at a range of ideas associated with critical thinking, particularly those linked with learning and development. It aims to present a number of ideas which should assist you in initially developing your knowledge and abilities within your study area. You are all unique learners and practitioners working in very different professional contexts so we have included a number of questions and activities to help you develop your own ideas and perspectives on this material. If you wish to enhance your understanding further in a particular area you will find suggested titles for further reading provided at the end of each chapter.

Second edition

This second edition has been updated to take account of the revised PQ framework and associated group of awards. As ever, it aims to provide help and guidance for qualifying and post-qualifying education but also aims to be of value to all social care practitioners.

A new chapter has been included to encompass the requirement for 'enabling others' in all PQ specialist awards, and to take account of continuing learning and professional development. This chapter discusses ways in which learning and development can be facilitated in the workplace to encourage a more critical approach.

Other sections have been expanded where we have had requests for more information, i.e. the nature of arguments; academic writing; professional knowledge and learning.

Chapter 1
Who is this handbook for?

How can the handbook help with qualifying and post-qualifying learning?

This handbook is written primarily for post-qualifying students but there are a number of ways in which critical thinking, particularly when associated with reflection and experiential learning, becomes an essential part of learning and development on qualifying as well as post-qualifying programmes. The aims and intended learning outcomes of such programmes and the requirements for continuing professional development show us how.

Qualifying programmes

In 2003, professional qualifying training for social workers in the United Kingdom changed from diploma to an undergraduate degree level. Qualities such as working in complex situations, exercising powers and responsibilities, managing risk and making informed decisions are all listed as final-year undergraduate assessment standards. These qualities involve various aspects associated with critical thinking, for example, reflection and sound deliberation, which in turn enable the application and development of knowledge and skills in the workplace. This is particularly pertinent now that qualifying students are expected to complete 200 days' practice learning taking place at practice sites. These placements are aimed at facilitating the development of social work skills, knowledge, critical analysis and evidence-based application of knowledge through work-based learning experiences. Developing critical thinking abilities and attributes can particularly help qualifying students extract and express in writing the learning and professional development occurring during their placements.

PQ specialist awards

The PQ specialist award is set at an equivalent standard of a final-year honours undergraduate degree (level H). Developing critical-thinking abilities and attributes can particularly help qualified social workers consolidate, extend and deepen their initial professional competence in a specialist context. In particular, the General Social Care Council (GSCC) requires specialist award students to:

> Use reflection and critical analysis to continuously develop and improve their specialist practice, including their practice in inter-professional and inter-agency contexts, drawing systematically, accurately and appropriately on theories, models and relevant up-to-date research.
> (GSCC, 2005, p16)

PQ higher specialist and advanced awards

The minimum academic level for these PQ awards is level M, equivalent to Masters level in higher education. Firstly, the higher specialist award has a specific focus on the knowledge and skills needed to make complex judgements and discharge high levels of responsibility for the co-ordination of social support and management of risk. This level is associated with professional issues involving complex problem solving and critical thinking, but will not involve an assessed research project. If undertaken as a stand-alone qualification it will normally be offered at postgraduate diploma level.

Secondly, the advanced award is focused on the knowledge and skills required for professional leadership, 'mastery' of a specific area of work, and improvement of services, and will build on and incorporate higher specialist work, leading to a Masters degree. Another feature of this level is a focus on developing the capacity to evaluate and undertake assessed research to support the ongoing improvement of services.

The GSCC state students undertaking M-level awards should:

> Demonstrate a full-developed capacity to use (and at advanced level take responsibility for the use of) reflection and critical analysis to continuously develop and improve own performance and the performance of professional and inter-professional groups, teams and networks; analysing, evaluating and applying relevant and up-to-date research evidence including service user research.
> (GSCC, 2005, p18)

Continuing learning

The GSCC's continuing professional development agenda for registered social workers consists of post-registration training and learning (PRTL) requirements, which act as a key condition for continued registration. During each three-year registration period, 90 hours or 15 days of study, training, courses, seminars, reading, teaching or other activities (for example, structured refection on practice) which could reasonably be expected to advance the social worker's professional development or contribute to the development of the profession as a whole, should be recorded and evidenced. The GSCC state that PRTL can be part of everyday practice, not something done separately but something reflected upon constantly. Guidance is available from the GSCC website (www.gscc.org.uk).

Rolfe et al. (2001) show that developing practice and learning cannot be separated. The development of practise is an ongoing activity; it generates experiential knowledge and so to practise is also to learn. The process and outcomes of continuing learning, when meaningfully achieved, will almost naturally embed themselves into processes of working, for example, with clearer thinking, writing, reflective analysis and evaluation. The most important learning, however, is meta-learning – that is learning about how you learn – and this is the basis of lifelong learning. This handbook, therefore, also focuses on learning as an end in itself and makes critical thinking and practice an integrated way of continuing to develop.

How can the handbook help with practice?

Social work as a profession has always demanded critical abilities and qualities from its practitioners because decisions have to be made 'on the spot' and under pressure. With practice situations being so complex, the consequences of any decisions and action are extremely important. The practitioner is working with uncertainty, risk, diversity and difference in a way that recognises oppression, and works to empower and promote the needs and rights of users and carers. This requirement goes beyond 'competent practice' and demands 'critical practice' (Adams et al., 2002), and the development of 'critical being', i.e. a person who not only reflects critically on knowledge but also develops their powers of critical self-reflection and critical action (Barnett, 1997).

No matter what we do, we cannot escape our thinking but it can often be left unquestioned in our busy lives. We suggest that developing critical thinking can ensure that we use the best thinking we are capable of in any set of circumstances.

Chapter 2
Critical thinking

ACHIEVING POST QUALIFYING SOCIAL WORK AWARDS

This chapter will help you to meet the following National Occupational Standards for Social Work.

- Key role 5: Unit 14: Manage and be accountable for your own work
- Key role 6: Unit 20: Manage complex ethical issues, dilemmas and conflicts.

If you are a registered social worker, this chapter will also assist you to evidence post-registration training and learning. It relates to the national post-qualifying framework for social work education and training, in particular the national criteria at the specialist level:

(ii) Think critically about their own practice in the context of the GSCC *Codes of Practice*, national and international codes of professional ethics and the principles of diversity, equality and social inclusion in a wide range of situations, including those associated with inter-agency and inter-professional work.

Aspects of critical thinking are apparent when you consider, deliberate, assess, make decisions and discuss or debate issues with others, so most social workers have plenty of skills and experience to build on. We are, therefore, not aiming to teach or present a set of separate techniques but to start you working with some relevant, generic ideas and principles which can develop your own style of critical thinking further.

We do not intend to cover the full range of critical-thinking 'skills' but instead highlight a few basic principles to underpin the process of enhancing the critical aspects of your own learning and development.

What's it all about?

Brookfield (1987) shows that critical thinking is a lived and creative activity, not an academic pastime.

Being a critical thinker involves more than cognitive activities such as logical reasoning or scrutinising arguments for assertions unsupported by empirical evidence. Thinking critically involves our recognising the assumptions underlying our beliefs and behaviours. It means we can give justifications for our ideas and actions. Most important, perhaps, it means we try to judge the rationality of these justifications. We can do this by comparing them to a range of varying interpretations and perspectives. We can think through, project, and anticipate the consequences of those actions that

are based on these justifications. And we can test the accuracy and rationality of these justifications against some kind of objective analysis of the 'real' world as we understand it.
(Brookfield, 1987, pp13–14)

Thinking critically can, therefore, result in major shifts in our ways of thinking and the development of reflective scepticism, i.e. when nothing is regarded as a universal truth, or taken on trust anymore. Our assumptions and beliefs, the views of others, and existing structures all start to be questioned, no matter what their basis or authority. It is powerful and transformative stuff and the challenge can be extremely positive. However, critical thinking can also be threatening, provoke anxiety and create adverse reactions from other people. It is hard work, involving self-doubt and mental blocks, but for many it leads to more creative leaps and insights. If you find yourself being adversely affected by the negative aspects, we advise you to seek support.

Critical thinking should not produce cynics but confident people who can be committed to a point of view that is well informed, rational and supported by relevant and valid material for that situation, but also open to other ideas. These are the type of social workers that the public deserve.

How can it be achieved?

Because people vary according to their capacities, abilities and experience, how you think critically will be personal to you. To develop this individuality we need an appropriate theory to provide us with valid and useful goals, methods and outcomes, i.e. an underpinning framework and structure. We propose to initially approach the 'how' in our context by using the theory of Bailin et al. (1999), who suggest that the critical thinker can be thought of in terms of a set of *requisite intellectual resources*. These ideas have been used successfully by Ford et al. (2004, 2005) in their research on criticality with students in social work education, and are explored below:

The intellectual resources for critical thinking are:

1. background knowledge;

2. critical concepts;

3. critical thinking standards;

4. strategies;

5. habits of mind.

We will look at each of these resources in turn and examine their components, why they are thought to be necessary, where and how they might be of use. We can also identify the ones we need to develop further.

Background knowledge of the situation in question

Bailin et al. (1999, p290) propose that:

> *the depth of knowledge, understanding and experience persons have in a particular area of study or practice is a significant determinant of the degree to which they are capable of thinking critically in that area.*

In other words, the more you know about your own situation, and the context in which it sits, the better. This includes existing concepts, beliefs, values and ways of acting, as well as the usual background information which helps clarify the range of available options, e.g. for assessment purposes. However, professional judgement is required to make an informed decision about the actual use of this material. Thus, 'context' plays a significant role in determining what will count as sensible or reasonable application of any standards and principles of critical thinking. This contextually sensitive and moral approach appears well suited to the social work arena and allows for responsible deliberation.

QUESTIONS

You don't know what you don't know, so how do you ensure that you are not missing something important about a practice situation?

How do you find out more – who and what are your sources?

Possession of critical concepts

In order to deliberate responsibly, and appraise all the material or information we are presented with, we need to understand the ideas and language (the concepts) associated with critical thinking. It is too easy to limit thinking about practice to thinking only of practice – that is, we get wrapped up in the detail and specifics of particular reasons, decision and actions, rather than dealing with their more general underlying traits. For example, an individual practitioner may reflect on a particular judgement concerning a foster carer by reviewing the available data and decision trail but miss out the possible effect of 'confirmation bias' (the tendency for the human mind to search for or interpret information in a way that confirms preconceptions) and thus not realise that a 'team view' on the case was being followed uncritically.

New knowledge concerning critical thinking allows us to become more aware of these underlying traits, and certain natural human tendencies towards bias, that we would normally not even recognise. This type of knowledge does run into areas of psychology and human behaviour but we do not need to study a new discipline here. For much of the time the key is to be able to dig deep enough and be honest enough to truly recognise the underlying preconceptions and assumptions we have.

Many authoritative websites explain a range of relevant cognitive and behavioural biases. Here are a few examples.

- *Anchoring effect* – tendency to rely too heavily or 'anchor' on one trait or piece of information when making decisions.

- *Bandwagon effect* – tendency to do or believe things because others do.

- *Confirmation bias* – tendency to search or interpret information in a way that confirms one's preconceptions.

- *Outcome bias* – tendency to judge a decision by its eventual outcome rather than the quality of the decision at the time it was made.

- *Pseudocertainty effect* – tendency to make risk-averse choices if the expected outcome is positive, but make risk-seeking choices to avoid negative outcomes.

Basic concepts regarding all arguments

Critical-thinking knowledge can be largely concerned with distinguishing and understanding various kinds of argument (e.g. Gibbs and Gambrill, 1999; Cottrell, 2005). Although this can be viewed as a more academic and mechanistic exercise, it does allow us to realise how easily we accept flawed arguments that others present to us. We can become more aware of how arguments work and develop the language to critique them properly rather than just 'feeling' there was something wrong with them.

Before we can fully appraise someone's argument, we first need to know which type of argument it is, and secondly have a full understanding regarding the various parts of an argument to make appropriate distinctions and judge it. Arguments are used to suggest the truth or demonstrate the falsity of a particular claim.

Logical arguments

Logical arguments are composed of propositions, i.e. claims that are capable of being either true or false, and can serve as the objects of belief – they are the building blocks. The propositions used as reasons or evidence within the argument become the argument's premises. They are the evidence or reasons for accepting the argument and its conclusion (the final proposition). There is a movement from one or more propositions used as premises to the proposition argued for as the conclusion, as in the following example.

- *This bookcase is wood* – proposition/premise.

- *Wood is a strong material* – proposition/premise.

- *The bookcase will support my heavy books* – final proposition/conclusion.

The premises must be true and 'accepted' and the relevance to the conclusion must be adequately supported by them. Premises will differ in their acceptability and credibility, and, therefore, in their sufficiency to support the conclusion. Any proposition also already carries with it other accepted positions, assumptions or 'givens', that are not always made explicit. For example, a premise that states *This country needs educated citizens to develop* will have a set of assumptions about what a 'citizen' should be or do, and about the role of the education system.

The connection between the propositions is called an *inference*. With inference, one proposition is arrived at on the basis of one or more other propositions already accepted. The problem is that inferences, by their nature, are not made explicit and so they have to be uncovered and identified in order to be critically examined. In the example above, the inference could be that the wood the bookshelf is made out of is the right quality for the weight of the books.

Types of logical argument – deductive and inductive

Deductive arguments The appropriate logical sequence for a deductive argument moves from the general to the specific. A *valid argument* here is defined as one where the argument's structure actually works as a sequence, even though the propositions (as premises or conclusion) may be false. A *sound argument* is a valid argument whose premises are all true and so it always arrives at a true conclusion. Be careful not to confuse valid arguments with sound arguments.

Example – valid but unsound deductive argument. One of the premises is false and so the conclusion is false. However, if the premises were all true then the conclusion would be true because the structure works as a sequence, and so the argument itself remains a valid one.

Premise: All tigers are blue.
Premise: The animal outside my window is a tiger.
Conclusion: The tiger outside my window is blue.

So it is important to note the fact that just because a deductive argument is valid, it does not imply that its conclusion holds true.

Example – valid and sound deductive argument. The premises are true, the conclusion is true and the argument is valid and sound.

Premise: All pilots are people who know how to fly airplanes.
Premise: John is a pilot.
Conclusion: John knows how to fly airplanes.

Example – invalid deductive argument. The premises are all true but the conclusion is false and so the argument is invalid.

Premise: Fish can swim.
Premise: My father can swim.
Conclusion: My father is a fish.

How does this happen? It is usually because of the hidden inferences and assumptions we mentioned above. This refers to anything that is taken for granted, e.g. facts, ideas or beliefs, which underlie the argument. For a deductive argument to have a justifiable conclusion (be sound as well as valid) not only must its premises be true, but the inferences which underlie them must also be reasonable and justifiable. As we said, a deductive argument infers from the general to the specific. This is where the problem occurs because other factors in a general statement might be present but not acknowledged. Our example inferred that anything that swims must be a fish. We could have worded the proposition as '*only fish can swim*' and then it would have been a valid argument at least, although obviously unsound!

Let's look at a more relevant example (from Gibbs and Gambrill, 1999):

Premise: John has an attention-deficit hyperactivity disorder.
Premise: This disorder decreases academic performance.
Premise: Drug x reduces hyperactivity in school children.
Conclusion: If we prescribe drug x for John, his academic performance will improve.

QUESTION

What are the inferences here?

ACTIVITY **2.1**

Write out a deductive argument using premises and conclusions from a practice example.

What are the inferences or assumptions?

Inductive arguments An inductive argument usually argues and infers from the specific to the general; i.e. the opposite way to a deductive argument. An inductive argument is one where the premises provide some evidence for the truth of the conclusion. Inductive arguments are not valid or invalid. This means that if the premises are true in an inductive argument then it is probable that the conclusion is true, but it might not be. Inductive reasoning consists of inferring from the properties of a sample to the properties of a population as a whole and works with the notion of probabilities.

For example, suppose we have a container containing 1,000 beads. Some of the beads are red and some of the beads are blue. If we take a sample of 100 beads from the container and 50 of them are red and 50 of them are blue, then we could infer inductively that half the beads in the container are red and half are blue. In all probability we are likely to be about right, but we could also be very wrong. Inductive reasoning also depends on the similarity of the sample and the population. The more similar the sample is to the population as a whole, the more reliable will be the inductive inference. No inductive inference is perfect and any one can fail. So, even though the premises are true, the conclusion might be false. Nonetheless, a good inductive inference will give us reason to believe that the conclusion is probably true.

Many general medical and social work theories are based upon observations of very specific experiments with samples. In our deductive example one of the premises was based on such a theory: *Drug x reduces hyperactivity in school children*. However, as we know, experiments cannot take into account all circumstances or situations (i.e. the evidence is incomplete). To see if this was an acceptable inductive conclusion in its own right it would be necessary to see whether the experiments with drug x were tested with a similar sample of children to John.

In another childcare context, Bowlby's findings (1951, 1969) suggested that infants who were separated from their mothers at an early age had behavioural and emotional difficulties later. This was used to argue the case against mothers working outside the home. This conclusion no doubt suited the economic conditions at the time; however, data was based on children in very extreme institutionalised situations and one could argue that these were not 'typical' children. So the conclusion may not have been justified even though the research was accurate. Research usually progresses in this way, with later researchers questioning aspects such as whether the sample was representative or whether the research contained assumptions invisible at the time (Cottrell, 2003).

ACTIVITY **2.2**

Do you know of any other social work theories that have been based on inductive reasoning?
Why are they considered probably true?

Knowledge of critical thinking standards

Once basic critical knowledge (the ideas and language) are understood we need practical methods to help us be critical about something. We need standards that will enable us to deliberate and judge effectively. Standards of critical assessment are specific for each area of activity, i.e. standards for criticising an argument will be different to those used for criticising a piece of research. There are two overlapping aspects to be aware of. Firstly, there are standards that allow us to judge a 'product' itself (e.g. a set of research findings, a decision outcome); and secondly, there are guiding principles that are relevant to the deliberation or inquiry undertaken to produce the product (e.g. the research methods, the decision-making process).

Standards and principles do not always guide a thinker on how to apply them because they are generalised from good practice itself. However, their abstractness gives them a vagueness that makes it necessary for the critical thinker to exercise judgement in interpreting them and determining what they require in any particular case – which is how it should be, if you think about it. The way in which you exercise this judgment and interpret the relevant standards and principles gives you important material for discussion on your programme. The worst way to use them would be as unexamined tick-box lists.

Developing such judgement is like learning a language – you don't follow an exact set of rules in speech, but you can act in a way the principles prescribe (e.g. using unambiguous words and short sentences) and recognise when your thinking fulfils these relevant standards (e.g. other people understanding you, rules of grammar). For example, in practice you may know you made a sound decision by following the right principles (e.g. involving all the relevant stakeholders, finding out background information, challenging your assumptions, etc.). You could also check the soundness of your process by measuring how well the outcome of the decision actually achieved its goals, or by evaluating how far your action is seen as ethical in the eyes of others outside the profession.

Presented below are the generalised standards relevant for the critical appraisal of assumptions, arguments, decisions, theory and research. These obviously need to be kept under review to ensure they are appropriate for each particular context.

Generally, we have seen that one of the overriding aspects of critical thinking is the questioning and checking of assumptions (e.g. to avoid cognitive and behavioural bias). To assume anything is to accept it without proof, so the posing of certain questions can start us unearthing and examining the issue to check its 'acceptability'. It is usually more effective if someone else questions us because we all come with our own blocks and barriers to this process. The point overall is to raise our awareness of aspects of ourselves that are usually subconscious, but which still have power to impact heavily on our thought processes and our more conscious decisions and actions. They may be positive as well as negative. The issue of negativity is dealt with later in the book.

Critical appraisal of assumptions

- What reasons/values/attitudes are these ideas/opinions/claims based on? Do they relate to a specific culture or group? Would they relate to others?

- What are the underlying perceptions, situational 'givens'?

- Are the ideas/opinions/claims accepted because they confirm what is thought rather than having valid evidence for this situation?

- Which situations do they apply to, and which would they not apply to?

QUESTIONS

Where do you exercise your critical judgement in the workplace?

Which standards or guiding principles do you to apply?

What assumptions have you come across recently? How did you question them?

Critical appraisal of arguments

There are a number of ways an argument or its reasoning may be flawed, such as:

- assuming that because two things are found together or occur at the same time, there must be a link between them;

- assuming there is a causal link between trends that are related;

- using false analogies;

- stereotyping;

- using emotive language.

Critical analysis of deductive arguments (from Gibbs and Gambrill, 1999)

- Does the conclusion have at least one premise in support of it?

- Are all the premises relevant to the truth of the conclusion? A premise is only acceptable if it:
  - is a matter of undisputed common knowledge;
  - can be adequately defended;
  - is the conclusion of another good argument;
  - is an incontrovertible eyewitness testimony;
  - is an unconvertible report from an expert in the field;
  - is different from the conclusion itself;
  - does not contradict the evidence, a well-established claim, a reliable source or other premises in the same argument;
  - is not self-contradictory, linguistically confusing or unintelligible.

- When viewed together, do the premises constitute sufficient grounds for the truth of the conclusion, strong enough in number, weight and kind? (Small and/or unrepresentative samples, or anecdotal evidence would be considered weak.)
- Do the premises provide an effective rebuttal to all reasonable challenges to the argument? This is a good criterion for distinguishing mediocre arguments, because many people ignore or hide contrary evidence. Good arguers examine counterarguments as well as compatible ones.

A deductive argument may be unsound because:

- there may be something wrong with its logical structure, e.g. when the conclusion does not follow on logically from the reasons preceding it and the inferences are weak;
- it contains 'false' (irrelevant, unacceptable, weak) premises;
- it bases conclusions on too little evidence (generalising from incomplete information) or overlooks alternative conclusions.

Critical analysis of inductive arguments

- The size of the sample should not be too small to support the conclusion.
- The sample used should not be relevantly different from the population as a whole.
- Any analogies must be valid. For example, it is argued that since A has property P, so also B must have property P. An analogy fails when the two objects, A and B, are different in a way which affects whether they both have property P.
- Important evidence which would undermine an inductive argument should not be excluded from consideration. The requirement that all relevant information be included is called the 'principle of total evidence'.

Critical appraisal of decisions
(using the decision-making framework from O'Sullivan, 1999, p20)

- Considering the decision-making contexts.
- Involving the client.
- Meeting with all stakeholders.
- Thinking and feeling about the decision situation.
- Framing the decision situation.
- Choosing an option.
- Evaluating soundness, viability and outcomes.

Critical appraisal of theories
(from Newman, c2000)

- According to this theory, what determines human behaviour?
- What are the major beliefs of the theory; which do I accept and why? Which don't I accept and why?
- Are the assumptions clearly defined, reasonable, ethically and socially consistent with my own and social work's assumptions and values?
- How applicable is the theory across settings, different clients, and problems?
- Is the theory clear, easy to understand and logical?

- Does the theory address cultural, ethical or racial issues? Is it culturally sensitive?
- What is the empirical (testable) support for the theory?
- Is it original?
- How does the theory compare and contrast with other theoretical approaches?

Critical appraisal of research evidence
(from Newman, c2000)

Look for:

- closeness to truth (validity);
- authority;
- relevance;
- outcomes;
- usefulness (applicability).

This critical appraisal of research evidence requires some specialist training, but these questions start you off.

- Have the authors clearly explained the purpose of the study, how it was carried out and the results?
- How confident can we be that the study sample is representative of the broader population – or does it relate to my clients?
- Did some people 'drop out' of the study, and if so, have the authors accounted for this in their conclusions?
- Have the authors showed how the findings were 'worked out'?
- Have the authors any reason to be biased?
- Are the claims made by the study plausible?
- Does the study add anything to what we already know?

The main question has to be – can it work in my situation?

Knowledge of strategies, and ways to find things out for oneself

People discover or devise key strategies and procedures for guiding their performance in a variety of thinking tasks, e.g. making lists of pros and cons for decision-making; using examples for clarifying terms; discussing issues with a knowledgeable person. Specific strategies tend to be more helpful than those designed to apply in all cases. What is most helpful is when they are shared among people struggling with the same issue.

ACTIVITY **2.3**

List some strategies or tips you already have for practice, e.g. making decisions, problem-solving; and for learning, e.g. reading, studying.

These ideas are great to share in groups. How can you create an opportunity to share ideas on your course or programme – over coffee, via email?

Habits of mind

As Bailin et al. (1999, p294) point out, having all the intellectual resources necessary for critical thinking does not make anyone a critical thinker. The final resource is probably the most important of them all. We need to have certain commitments, attitudes or habits (e.g. respect for reason and truth; an open rather than a defensive attitude) and recognise the value of critical thinking in fostering true belief and responsible action as well. These attributes are closely tied up with our ethics and values. Social work, with its interdisciplinary nature and its inherent value system guiding judgement and action, is obviously well placed for fostering such habits of mind, but it is easy to become complacent and believe they are occurring automatically. Chapter 6 looks more closely at how routine practice easily becomes uncritical and even arrogant practice.

In practice we need knowledge about the subject at hand, self-knowledge (an honest recognition of how we think and reason), plus a range of values, attitudes and dispositions related to personal humility, human rights and the dignity and intrinsic worth of all human beings. These attributes underpin the ability to practise critically and encourage the inherent requirements of social work: openness, questioning and responsibility.

QUESTION

Which specific social work (or other practice) values do you think are relevant for critical thinking?

Review

We have chosen to use one set of critical thinking ideas to develop in this section but you will probably find other authors' work echoing this material. For example, Smith (1992) identifies three key factors in critical thinking: knowledge, authority and a willingness to doubt. *Knowledge* fits exactly with our first intellectual resource of background knowledge; *authority* would involve the use of our critical concepts, standards and strategies; and a *willingness to doubt* would be our habit of mind.

As we can see, critical thinking cannot be thought of as something that finds perfect solutions. Rather, the skills of critical thinking allow the best-quality decisions or actions possible for the situations we encounter. Our holistic view advocates not just the application of critical-thinking principles and techniques, but a more developed understanding of how our thinking operates in our day-to-day environments and the dangers we need to become more aware of.

ACTIVITY **2.4**

Developing critical thinking about the statements we make
Terms such as 'value', 'empirical', 'conceptual', 'causal' might seem rather academic but they refer to the types of statements used in general speech and when arguing for social care resources. For example:

This child needs help because …

- he is not in the right type of environment. *A value statement – values are different for everyone.*

- he has injuries. An empirical statement – *these injuries should be in evidence and thus are verifiable (testable).*

- he is unhappy. *A conceptual statement – because concepts are ideas that relate to a class of objects they are not specific.*

- if we leave him he will be subject to more abuse. *A causal statement – assumes one thing affects another.*

We therefore need to be able to recognise and effectively appraise each of these types of statements.

You might use our reading list below to find out more or use a search engine like Google (www.google.co.uk) on the Internet for general resources. Just make sure you look at authoritative sources.

Social work resources concentrate on critical evaluation of research and include the following:

Research in Practice *www.rip.org.uk/ and www.ripfa.org.uk*
RIP promotes positive outcomes for children and families, and for adults through the use of research evidence. Their learning resources concentrate on current research and how to apply it to practice and provide skills development opportunities for improving evidence-informed practice.

Research Mindedness *www.resmind.swap.ac.uk/*
Research Mindedness helps students and practitioners of social care and social work make greater and more effective use of research in their studies and in practice.

The PQ framework will provide many opportunities to use these critical-thinking principles – in applying your new knowledge into practice, in reflecting on learning and practice, when writing, and when continuing learning. We will now explore each of these areas in turn and develop the notion of critical thinking within them.

URTHER
EADING

Brookfield, S (1987) *Developing critical thinkers*. Milton Keynes: Open University Press. A general but insightful look at becoming a critical person.

Fisher, A (2001) *Critical thinking. An introduction*. Cambridge: Cambridge University Press. Excellent for specific critical-thinking concepts and techniques.

O'Sullivan, T (1999). Decision making in social work. London: Macmillan. Critical thinking within a specific process.

Chapter 3

Learning – applying new knowledge to practice

The PQ framework will introduce you to theory and research in the specialist area of your choice. The application of external or theoretical knowledge to practice will usually be an active and important learning experience because such knowledge cannot usually be applied systematically or predictably, and things won't necessarily go according to plan. In other words, it will be steep learning curve. Developing practice by applying or even just linking new ideas and knowledge is one of the most important ways critical thinking can be practised in the workplace (Argyris and Schön, 1974).

Applying theory and research

If we look at these processes more closely, we can see that theory and research findings can only inform; they cannot predict or control exactly what will take place. Research evidence can be extremely useful material for social workers (especially newly qualified) to gain more information about issues, possible interventions and outcomes, but they cannot be taken 'off the shelf' as an unmediated solution, or be seen to exactly 'match' a specific situation. In fact, it would be difficult to reduce the complex, uncertain and unstable situations we work with to something that a standardised theoretical body of knowledge, or a set of specific research findings, can answer (Adams et al., 2002). External knowledge will need to be internalised and processed first – i.e. adapted for specific and unique conditions, and integrated with experience and values as well. These adaptation and integration processes can be linked to learning and the development of professional expertise.

The process of adaptation may allow some of the original ideas, rules or procedures to remain relatively intact, but more often they may be interpreted further and then combined with other ideas, information and knowledge. This process also aligns with the way we learn. Learning is usually about fitting new material into existing material and involves the processes of abstracting general principles from the new ideas so that they can be matched with, or connected to, the knowledge we already have (Sotto, 1994). Only then is it ready to be transferred effectively to a new situation.

As Race (2001) puts it, the abstracting of principles or generalising involves a lot of 'digesting', which means:

- sorting out what is important;
- extracting fundamental principles;
- discarding what is not important;
- establishing a sense of ownership of it.

There is no model or process for how external knowledge is mediated or generalised to make it relevant and useful. Such a transfer of knowledge isn't an exact or linear process, but as practitioners we are constantly building on and using our inputs of information and knowledge whether we are fully aware of it or not. Secker's (1993) work is particularly useful in this area. However, using new knowledge gained from an academic environment for practice is at first conscious and deliberative. There are a number of difficulties. For example, theories and research may be viewed by practitioners as unchallengeable wisdom. To criticise this type of information might seem presumptuous but it is important for practitioners to show how knowledge meant for practice can be used for specific situations and how it actually 'performs' when used. In this way, a practitioner's voice can develop its own authority.

From a critical-thinking perspective the process of applying new knowledge into practice may require a framework to ensure certain activities are covered which provide the process with a necessary robustness and validity. In other words, we are trying to ensure that is not merely a trial-and-error exercise. Presented in Table 3.1 is a framework for applying new knowledge into practice with associated general assessment headings for this level of work (QAA, 2001). Such a framework will also help ensure that the process ultimately addresses situation-focused needs, and allows you to demonstrate the criteria on which you are likely to be marked for degree-level work.

Table 3.1 Framework for applying new knowledge to practice with associated assessment headings

Activities associated with applying new knowledge in practice	General assessment headings
A. Understand the practice situation, issue or problem	*Identification, definition, comprehension, diagnosis*
B. Identify and judge new and relevant general, underlying principles/elements from external sources for use	*Comprehension, analysis, critical appraisal*
C. Combine principles with experience, ideas and values	*Transformation of abstract data and concepts, creativity*
D. Design solution and apply to a new situation, or align with a past experience	*Design, creativity, transfer*
E. Critically monitor, judge or measure strategy, progress and outcome/s	*Critical evaluation*

Obviously, this process involves more than a straightforward or linear application of particular technical skills and is a highly reflective experience, generating a practitioner's own knowledge for practice. Responsible assessment and deliberation will also be very apparent throughout the process, as well as other more implicit and less conscious elements, for example-perception, interpretation, emotion, reflection. We will deal with the reflective element later in the handbook.

If we revisit our set of 'intellectual resources' for critical thinking in the previous section, we can see various alignments. Overall, the framework presented here can be seen to provide a number of critical-thinking strategies. More specifically, critical thinking concepts and standards would be applied in area B in Table 3.1, to allow critical appraisal of any theory, etc.

QUESTION

Where else in this framework would critical-thinking intellectual resources be used and how?

Application of practice knowledge

Working critically with new knowledge

Novice practitioners may be more comfortable working with known knowledge (e.g. theory) rather than unknown (e.g. a new case assessment) due to their lack of an established frame of reference built upon experience. Application of theory at this level, therefore, tends to be deductive, i.e. working from the generalised aspects of known theories and frameworks and applying them to a particular situation. The issue here is that these abstract theories may be imposed on new situations in order to understand them, and the inherent meaning of the situation (usually contained within the detail) may be lost when trying to produce rational solutions. In effect, the situation may become manipulated to fit the template of the theory, which distorts true understanding.

Instead, Margetson (2000, cited Nixon and Murr, 2006, p807) advocates an inductive approach, where reasoning is developed first from observed examples with reference back to theoretical knowledge. This enables more interpretive habits and in turn allows for complexity and creativity to be taken into account. The inductive approach allows for a reinterpretation of meaning in new contexts rather than imposition of one truth across contexts, and for Fook et al. (2000, p191) becomes *contextual theory development*. Our framework for applying new knowledge to practice (Table 3.1) is based on a more inductive approach and starts with an understanding of the practice situation.

Lester (1995) has argued that it is no longer adequate to base professional development on transmitting existing knowledge or developing a predefined range of competences. He wants practitioners to be able to construct and reconstruct the knowledge and skills they need and continually evolve their practice, in order to respond intelligently to unknown situations and go beyond established knowledge to create unique interpretations and outcomes. His model is not just concerned with logic but with values and perspective as well. The expert 'skill' lies in being able to theorise the situation first in order to construct the problem to be solved. Key tools are synthesis, situational and ethical understandings, and the ability to interpret the meanings of situations from a range of perspectives and standpoints, as well as analysis and expert knowledge. What we have as a result is not a reduced concept of professional expertise but an appreciation of the divergent but also holistic, interconnected and value-based nature of situations and problems.

The creation of such professional knowledge from practice echoes earlier work by Schön (1983) and Eraut (1994), who advocate the support and guidance of practitioners through experience to understand and determine the value of this knowledge, and to critically evaluate the development of work-based theories. A recent review (Nixon and Murr, 2006) of thinking in this area for social work practice concluded that professional knowledge is created by the worker by combining and re-combining more explicit theoretical knowledge with an understanding of tacit or implicit knowledge from professional processes. This legitimate generation of 'practice theory' (where generated practice knowledge and wisdom are integrated with factual and theoretical knowledge to develop expert knowledge) can take fuller account of the complexity and uncertainty of practice. In this respect, professional knowledge becomes more holistic and concerned with 'being' rather than just knowing, and thus necessarily complex and extensive.

We can also see that this practice theory, once legitimately generated and evaluated, can become potent material for post-qualifying study and other CPD work. The articulation of such knowledge within assignments and portfolios creates the necessary confidence and 'voice' from which to argue and reason more coherently and robustly. It also works towards a clearer understanding of a practitioner's or team's *theories in use* (Argyris and Schön, 1974) which may be useful for team-based developmental activities.

Working critically with practice knowledge

Although many practitioners see their practice knowledge as intuitive and personal, and therefore unworthy of acknowledgement in an academic environment, it does not have to lack the rigour, testability or validity of academic knowledge if we can demonstrate critical awareness, validation and evaluation of it. Eraut (1994) in particular stated that professional education should not ignore the knowledge embedded in application and practice. Learning or developing practice knowledge can be haphazard and unplanned processes. But practice is not always idiosyncratic, or necessarily implicit. Whatever is consciously and intentionally performed as practice implies an underpinning set of principles being acted upon. These principles will usually be based upon theoretical knowledge, experience, as well as values, and are at the heart of the notion of expertise. Argyris and Schön (1974); Schön (1983, 1987) and Eraut (1994) all develop the meaning of practice knowledge further.

The main point is that many of these principles can be explored, and evidenced, by identifying and appraising the processes and content of our reasoning and actions. In fact, to be totally unaware of them would be tantamount to not taking responsibility for the effects of our actions, which is unacceptable in any profession. As professional knowledge depends on the range of contexts in which it is used and tested, we can begin to create powerful meanings from our accumulated experience for the purposes of the PQ framework. For many students the process of identifying, articulating and evaluating their practice knowledge has been a very empowering learning experience because they have begun to discover their own voice.

However, the articulation of developing practices may prove a challenge to those practitioners who have been out of formal education for a while. Trying to make our learning, experience and knowledge more explicit for the PQ framework is a major undertaking. We need to take extra time to examine more closely what we do, why we do it and what this means. One way of dealing with this is to use reflection, which is the subject of the next chapter.

FURTHER READING

Fisher, T and Somerton, J (2000) Reflection on action: the process of helping social workers to develop their use of theory in practice. *Social Work Education*, 19 (4), 387–401.

Pawson, R, Boaz, A, Grayson, L, Long, A and Barnes, C (2003) *Types and quality of knowledge in social care*. Knowledge Review No.3. London: SCIE

Secker, J (1993) *From theory to practice in social work. The development of social work students' practice*. Aldershot: Avebury.

Watson, F, Burrows, H, and Player, C (2002) *Integrating theory and practice in social work education*. London: Jessica Kingsley.

Chapter 4
Critical reflection

Critical thinking itself involves a reflective dimension and the idea of reflective learning is therefore closely connected to it (Brookfield, 1987). We may not always be sure about what reflection is (any more than we can fully understand what learning is) and Ixer (1999) in particular argues that we do not know enough about its processes to assess it validly. However, we can understand what it can do within our own context.

The PQ framework assesses the learning and development occurring within educational and practice settings. Being reflective will allow awareness, analysis and evaluation of these educational and practice-based experiences in order to fully realise, and better express, the knowledge gained and the learning and development that took place. The way you do this is a crucial factor in gaining any award.

Emphasis is placed not on a descriptive account of what happened but on a full-scale examination of the hows, whys and 'what it all means' for future practice. In order to do this we would need to reflect deeply and critically upon the experience or situation.

What is reflection?

When described in the literature, critical reflection is usually referred to as the thinking activities engaged in to critically analyse and evaluate experiences, producing outcomes of new understandings and appreciations of the way we think and operate. The concept of self-awareness is always apparent, which allows the subjective element (feelings and emotions associated with a situation) to be analysed and evaluated at the same time. The consideration of external knowledge to provide a broad and current context may also be included.

Schön (1983, 1987) developed ideas around two main types of reflection for practice.

- *Reflection on action* when we think back on something already done.
- *Reflection in action* when we think about what we are doing while we are doing it.

Even though he uses the same term, it would seem apparent that the processes are very different. When we are doing something, we rarely have the time or opportunity to be consciously deliberative or analytical, and so the manner of our 'reflection' is likely to be much more holistic, intuitive and automatic in the latter situation (Van Manen, 1995).

For the former situation (reflection on action) we can think of reflection as a developing personal ability. Everyone seems to adopt their own method to help it happen – some people like to keep a journal, others make jottings or notes, some draw pictures or mind-maps, and others just think in the bath. To do it effectively there are guidelines to follow, and deep and critical levels to achieve for PQ awards, and these will be explained below. All it takes is an ability to think, to be self-aware and to question – but it takes practice to develop a method suitable for you and attain the necessary level, as we don't always do this automatically. Practice needs time, commitment, and some support – these are the variables.

What does it achieve?

Your reflection will produce a lot of thoughts, ideas, connections and insights into your learning and development. This also follows Schön's (1987) ideas, which explore how professional expertise is developed through the use of critical reflection. Rather than repeating the same experience or developing your own implicit rules of thumb, etc., you can explore, understand and justify your practice deliberations, decisions and actions in different ways using critical intellectual resources and develop new perspectives for future practice using available theory, research, knowledge and experience.

To use the earlier language of Argyris and Schön (1974), we reveal our *theories-in-use* (the implicit theories that govern our actual behaviour and contain assumptions about self, others and environment) and examine them against our *espoused theory* (the words we use to convey what we do or what we would like others to think we do) to see if they fit. A small gap between the two might not be a bad thing but if it gets too wide then there is clearly a difficulty. Provided the two remain connected then the gap creates a dynamic for reflection and for dialogue.

However, our need goes beyond being a 'reflective practitioner' in a narrow sense. Because reflection for our purposes is in a social work education context, the main outcome of reflection is seen to be an identification and evaluation of the learning and development pertaining to future practice, i.e. the development of the self as a critical practitioner (Adams et al., 2002). The aim is to think beyond the acknowledgement and description of difficult aspects of a situation to an evaluation of how they were dealt with, i.e. the resulting action.

The overall standards of learning in this context are therefore change and development. These ideas are discussed in more depth by Mezirow et al. (1990) as the development of practice to oppose and redress power imbalances. The main outcome of critical reflection on practice in a social work context will therefore be an identification and evaluation of that learning and development relevant to values, as well as future practice methods.

Argyris and Schön (1974) call it *double-loop learning* when an 'error' is detected and corrected in ways that involve the modification of underlying norms, values and objectives, as well as the techniques or strategies. They argue that double-loop learning is necessary if practitioners are to make informed decisions in rapidly changing and often uncertain contexts. This learning should also encompass and, if possible, inform policy changes at organisational level where appropriate.

How far do we go with reflection?

Kolb (1984) initially created a model called the *experiential learning cycle*, where the learner changes from an active participant in an experience, to a reflector on it, then an analyst of it; and then onto an experimenter with new ideas for a new experience. Reflective learning for us goes further to draw out the complete 'learning' for the person and their practice from the experiential process, and links the critical incidents to ideas and theories which shed light on them (Beatty, 2003, cited Parker, 2004). So being reflective means exploring experiences (positive and negative, small or large) and moving into new understanding. New understanding is key feature of a deep approach to learning, as opposed to surface learning or memorising.

Reflective processes can guide our learning experiences during an event and they can also guide our ability to express or show how this change occurred after the event (Moon, 2001). Degree-level assignments might ask you to explore your reflections or thoughts before, during and after an experience. As we have already discussed, reflection in action is much more intuitive and so will be much harder to articulate later on. Taking the time and space to take a step back from an event, or adopting a helicopter view over it, may help you. Many students have said how reading up on a practice area also helps them clarify their thoughts.

The rule is that academic reflection usually has to show knowledge, critical thought, analysis and evaluation. Deeper levels of reflection will, therefore, gain more marks than shallow ones and we will now explore them in detail.

Levels of reflection

There are a number of models of reflection that can be followed to develop deeper levels and your choice will be a personal one. There are certain aspects common to most of these models and they have been collated and simplified below in Table 4.1 in a framework, again with the associated general assessment headings (QAA, 2001) show how they relate to the academic levels for PQ specialist award work.

Table 4.1 Framework of reflective levels with associated assessment headings for specialist awards

Key levels and aspects of reflection	General assessment headings
Description Show awareness of important and relevant aspects of self and the situation – include feelings and thoughts concerning complex issues and dilemmas. *What, who, when, where?*	*Identification, definition*
Critical analysis Explore parts and reasons – e.g. feelings, actions, decisions, links to literature, etc. Challenge or question underlying assumptions, knowledge, experience, etc. *How, why?*	*Analysis, critical appraisal*
Evaluation Judge input, deliberations, decisions and outcomes; include ideas, information, knowledge, experience, values, professional powers, risk. Show insight into relevant issues, wider contexts, different perspectives. *How well...? what about...?*	*Evaluation, judgement* *Insight, synthesis, creativity*
Learning Produce and evaluate new understandings, perspectives, creative/original solutions, development, change or learning for practice methods and values. *What does this mean?*	*Development of self and practice knowledge* *Personal responsibility* *Professional competencies*

Of course it is not possible to regard these levels as totally distinct or mutually exclusive and, as seen before, there are many other more implicit elements not included. However, we can revisit our intellectual resources for critical thinking and note various applications throughout.

Where do you think critical-thinking intellectual resources should be used within these levels and how?

In order to understand how the levels interrelate and lead on from one another we will look at an analogy – school science lessons. The way they were written up usually followed a format like this:

Example

Reflection on a science lesson

The order for the write-up

- **Apparatus**: What did we use? Test-tube, Bunsen burner, chemicals.
- **Method**: What did we do? The chemicals were heated in the test-tube over the Bunsen burner.
- **Results**: What happened? It went bang!
- **Conclusion**: Why did that happen? The flame was too high.

The apparatus, methods and results sections can be seen to echo the first level of reflection (description), i.e. they are a mere reporting of the facts about what was done and what happened. The experiment's conclusion, an investigation of why the result happened as it did, echoes the second stage of reflection (analysis). This 'uncovering' process would show the teacher how much understanding occurred. For example, did the pupils realise the chemicals reacted differently at different temperatures, etc.?

So this is where the reasons, the issues and factors behind what has happened are thought about in detail, and therefore hopefully uncovered, analysed and explained. It is easy to confuse the reporting of results with an understanding of conclusions. The observational process is important but understanding why something happened, rather than just knowing what happened, is an important stage in learning. However, deeper learning goes beyond this and involves further reflection and investigation.

The next level of reflection (evaluation) can only happen when the previous stage has taken place. In our example we know the flame was too hot and this caused the chemicals to explode but we need to know whether an explosion was our original aim or required outcome. If we did not want an explosion to happen, the outcome is deemed to be 'wrong' and we would want to make sure it didn't happen again. We therefore need to know why the flame was too hot. Further investigation might show that the air regulator on the Bunsen burner got stuck and couldn't be closed at the crucial moment in order to lower the heat of the flame. By looking deeper and enhancing our understanding of the situation we not only know how well we did, we also have new issues to reflect on. We can now use this new information to move onto the final stage.

The last level of reflection (learning) takes us into an area of thinking about the future and into action, i.e. what has been learnt, what does this mean, what changes are needed? In our classroom situation we might think that because the chemicals needed a low temperature it would be important to check the equipment before use next time and ensure the air regulator could be closed. This new understanding and learning would not have occurred without deeper reflection and evaluation of the original outcome.

Obviously this is a very simple analogy which does not include important aspects of self, context and values, but it shows how deeper and more critical reflection creates greater understanding and further learning.

ACTIVITY 4.1

Write out one of your own practice experiences using these levels, but try to include some of the aspects we missed, such as feelings/self; the wider context; values.

Reflection on some experiences may go even further and change deep and personally held beliefs, assumptions or inner values. If this happens you may need the extra support of someone you trust to help you deal with it, so it is important you recognise this as soon as it starts to happen.

Can it end up a bit negative?

It can feel negative when things we try in practice don't turn out the way we expect. We can start to feel anxious and defensive when having to think about it all again. But we are dealing with real life and your tutors will actually expect a conflict between prior expectations and experiences. What is required is that this conflict is not ignored or glossed over but explored further in order to develop practice. What is certain is that 'false accounts' of reflection are fairly easy to spot. If you are at all unsure about how much or what you are supposed to reveal, then ask your tutors to be as explicit as possible regarding what they are looking for. They should distinguish between what is deemed 'public information' and thus used for assessment, and what is personal and private.

Understanding new ideas can involve the reassessment of old perspectives, which can be discomforting, whereas exploring the things that have gone right can affirm and help understanding of experience and knowledge in more detail. But reflecting on all types of experiences (the negative and positive) can:

- allow greater awareness and expression of all types of learning and development
- show enhanced understanding from why things did work, as well as why they didn't

- provide a more positive ending for the negative experiences rather than just leaving things as they were, and allow a proper and full recognition of the good experiences and ones' strengths.

We also need to understand how to apply or transfer these strengths and work with our talents in new or more difficult situations. We already possess much of what we need to develop but a lot of it lies hidden or unrecognised unless it is reflected on. This is a *strengths-perspective* approach for enabling others. Reflection on problems can weaken confidence to develop in self-reflective ways (Weick et al., 1989) but a shift towards possibilities creates new, positive and individual paths for people. Learning to transfer strengths from one setting to another is a key component in lifelong learning.

However, placing oneself at the centre of an event or experience can lead to a pre-occupation with the self that can border on self-absorption. To avoid this happening, ensure that your reflection turns outwards as well, i.e. onto practice values, principles, traditions and the wider context relevant to the issue. Also be aware that reflection is not foolproof. Remembering the past is dependent on many different factors and is fallible. When an experience is reflected on, the original event becomes shaped and coloured by that reflection. Many courses advise the keeping of notes or a journal of some sort to record and preserve what actually happened and enable more accurate recall at a later date.

Other useful activities to develop reflection are questioning and sharing thoughts with others, which is why group work and communication with colleagues and fellow students is particularly important on the PQ framework.

Review

Reflecting deeply and critically is about making sure that all the aspects above are covered – i.e. there is an evaluated outcome or conclusion in terms of your understanding and learning and development. These ideas provide the necessary elements to write about in a PQ assignment but it is important to understand academic writing style in order to articulate ideas in the correct way. The following chapter will elaborate on this.

FURTHER READING

Moon, J, (1999b) *Reflection in learning and professional development: theory and practice.* London: Kogan Page.

Rolfe, G, Freshwater, D and Jasper, M (2001) *Critical reflection for nursing and the helping professions.* London: Palgrave.

Chapter 5
Writing reflective academic assignments

A C H I E V I N G   P O S T   Q U A L I F Y I N G   S O C I A L   W O R K   A W A R D S

This chapter will help you to meet the following National Occupational Standards for Social Work.

- Key role 6: Unit 18: Research, analyse, evaluate and use current knowledge of best social work practice
- Key role 6: Unit 19: Work within agreed standards of social work practice and ensure own professional development.

If you are a registered social worker, this chapter will also assist you to evidence post-registration training and learning. It relates to the national post qualifying framework for social work education and training in particular the national criteria at the specialist level:

(i) Meet the relevant academic standards associated with the subject of social work at this level.

This section focuses on reflective academic assignments and suggests ways to structure and write them using the guidelines we give our own students. Not all universities adopt this style of assignment for the PQ framework, and different institutions will assess reflective assignments in various ways for each of the academic levels, so it is necessary to check with your tutors before you follow the guidance given here. However, this guidance is based on years of teaching experience and of external assessment, so we feel confident of its value.

In general, the reflective assignment needs to show and evidence practice knowledge, the understanding and application of any theory or research, the learning outcomes achieved and professional development. It is, therefore, not a description of events or feelings. It should allow your learning derived from your critical thinking and reflection to be expressed.

How you view any assignment will depend on your previous experiences of education, and the length of time since being a formal 'learner', but it will be important not to make any assumptions and to follow your course handbooks and assignment guidelines very carefully.

Benefits of writing

Academic assessment can be dominated by written work. As with most qualifications, it is not what you think or do, but the way you articulate it that is graded. Assignment writing is, therefore, important because it is a major way in which existing or developing practice can be expressed for assessment purposes. This is a positive aspect because we understand and learn more while we are writing, as the process supports and develops reflective and critical abilities. It is also a skill social workers must acquire because it is often via written reports that clients are represented. This cannot be overstated. Good social work often requires the writing of reports for the benefit of the client and well-written reports will require the same skills.

According to Moon (1999a), writing:

- forces us to spend the time;
- helps us focus and sift material by slowing us down;
- forces us to organise and clarify our thoughts so we can sequence them;
- gives us a structure;
- gives control – we choose which points to make – and enables identification and prioritising of material;
- helps us to know if we do understand something by attempting to explain it;
- can help develop a deeper understanding of something as we work through it and explain it;
- can record a train of thought and relate it to the past, present and future;
- can initiate new ideas, connections, questions, etc.

Because critical reflection relies so much on making connections and judging our thoughts and information, writing is one of the main activities that can help by starting this process of capturing and expressing basic assumptions, underlying knowledge and the memory of any experience. Writing skills are primarily thinking skills but because writing is slower it can achieve more, especially in developing connections, exploring the experience more deeply, and gaining different perspectives.

Writing is not a one-off activity. All writing is about drafting and rewriting. It has a powerful effect in prompting further insights and hunches – the problem is that once we write these down, they sound clumsy. This is because these ideas come into our minds as holistic and compacted 'nuggets'. To convey them in structured language is like trying to translate them from one code into another. It won't happen in one or two attempts. Also, this translation process will throw up further ideas as we explore and unravel the original one. It is no wonder we go off on tangents and get lost! The key is to have a structure and a disciplined approach so that we can work with and control all these thoughts and articulate a clear message from them.

We wish to point out here that we believe PQ assignments need to be based on, and reflect, your practice – hence critical reflection. Society does not need social workers who can write theoretically about practice, but cannot practise competently or reflect on their own practice; society needs capable, skilled practitioners. In other words, society needs social workers who can critically reflect on their practice and debate and demonstrate competence and capability articulately.

Coverage

Choosing what to write about will obviously depend entirely on what the assignment is for but it will usually be concerned with new knowledge becoming embedded in practice.

A study of the assignment content guidelines and learning outcomes will identify all the areas to cover. Then you can decide which experiences or examples will be able to show and evidence these areas best; or plan for a new experience to allow this. List the areas the assignment wants you to cover. Then develop some ideas around them. How you do this is up to you; everyone has a different way, whether it's using lists or pictures. But do start – even if it's with *Once a upon a time…* . Only when something is down on paper or on a PC can you begin to work on it and make it better – if it's stuck in your head it's probably just going to float about doing nothing except worry you.

Using the reflective levels

As we have seen, reflecting in the PQ context is about concentrating on the deeper, critical levels, i.e. to ensure that there is an outcome in terms of your understanding, evaluation and learning about the education and practice events you are involved with. If we re-examine the reflective levels, we can see that the questions associated with each of them can also help develop our initial, often more descriptive, thoughts and reflections onto more analytical and evaluative levels. See Table 5.1.

Table 5.1 Questions to develop descriptive reflection

Description	Critical analysis	Evaluation	Learning
What did you do? What happened? What did you feel?	How did you do it? Why did you do it that way? Why did you not do it a different way?	How far and in what ways were your goals met? What other factors were apparent?	So what does this mean for future practice and your values?

We can go further and identify the type of material that might need to be included in answer to these questions at each level. See Table 5.2.

Table 5.2 Type of material to include at each reflective level

Description	Critical analysis	Evaluation	Learning
Background	Theory, research	Judgement, measurement of progress and outcome/s	Abstracting general principles
Context	Experience, practice knowledge	Strengths, weaknesses, gaps	Insights, ideas, new perspectives
Feelings	Values, ethics, conflicts	Counter arguments and theories	Synthesis with existing knowledge
Specific relevant details	Aims and objectives	Wider context, other factors	Professional development
Definitions	Judgements, assumptions	Different perspectives	Future planning, changes
	Decisions, deliberations; reflection 'before, in and after action'	Alternatives	Further theory, research

Table 5.2 mainly follows a 'reflection-on-action' idea (see Chapter 3; Schön, 1983) and a linear progression from left to right. It is not meant to be a prescriptive approach and you can use it in any way that helps. However, there is much this table cannot account for – i.e. the subtlety, depth, emotion and intuition involved in learning and thinking. Some of the questions or areas may not be relevant to your experience or reflection, and your own individual style and approach may require more holistic guidance to follow.

We are merely suggesting that reflective writing is a developmental and ongoing process, requiring time and feedback, and the elements noted above are all important aspects to be included because they are the elements usually being assessed for the PQ awards. At its heart, PQ specialist award study is about the demonstration of competence to practise and this cannot occur without reflection on your practice.

Structure – developing an argument

Stage 1: Developing a viewpoint and starting to make an argument

The starting point for structuring an assignment of this type is your overall point of view, or your basic 'claim'. You cannot really start writing a first complete draft until you know what it is you want to say. And you won't know this until all the stages of the reflection process, and initial reading of the subject area, have been achieved. Your viewpoint consists of what has been understood and learnt, plus what this means for your practice and values. A viewpoint forms the basis of your argument and allows you to control the material and develop your own voice. If you get stuck at this stage use Table 5.1, which may help you to reflect deeper. If you still feel lost, try discussing with a tutor. Even the smallest practice incidents can be packed with implicit new knowledge or learning but you may not be able see it for yourself without some critical questioning.

Developing the confidence to work with material in a way that allows your unique interpretation to be valued is a key underpinning aspect of degree-level work. As we have seen, recent literature concerning professional knowledge in social work emphasises the legitimate generation of *practice theory*, where generated practice knowledge and wisdom are integrated with factual and theoretical knowledge to develop expert knowledge which is able to take full account of the complexity and uncertainty of practice (e.g. Fook et al., 2000).

Here is a simplified example of a viewpoint.

> ### Example – assignment for a specialist area of social work: enabling others
>
> *Stage 1: My viewpoint*
>
> Good communication is essential when planning successfully for a placement student.
>
> *Notes:* I have learnt that because we need people in order to achieve things, communicating effectively helps us achieve more. This is another way we can show respect to others. The literature on placement planning generally agrees. Some authors do not give this area a lot of emphasis, though.

Stage 2: Reasons give the structure a sequence

Once your viewpoint is known, you can then focus any further reflection and research on the pivotal points (e.g. the events or specific instances in your learning experience) which have been instrumental in getting you here; i.e. the reasons behind how you got to this point of view. (You will start to recognise that you are forming your own set of propositions similar to more structured logical arguments.)

For a 5,000-word assignment you will probably only be able to focus effectively on three or four main reasons. Too often we pick a subject that is just too big. Focus down – this will give you space to be analytical and not descriptive. These reasons should be organised in a way that can best persuade your reader to agree.

By expressing your viewpoint and reasons in this way, you are making a claim to knowledge, but this will be viewed by the tutors as opinion only at this stage. In fact, it would also be viewed as opinion if we applied critical-thinking standards to such a claim. An experience does not automatically possess an innate validity and would, therefore, remain merely anecdotal without external connections. You now have to sustain this claim to knowledge in response to (or in anticipation of) a 'challenge' when you are in an academic environment. In other words you now have to show the validity of this view and your commitment to it. This is not unusual, unique or inappropriate – social workers are constantly justifying their decisions and actions when challenged by service users, or managers, or colleagues in practice.

In this context you back up your viewpoint and reasons by further researching the topic in the literature and offer reliable evidence or examples (either theory, research, or possibly other material such as case studies, practice guidance, policy, etc.) in support of your ideas. By showing where this evidence has come from (by citing and referencing it) you can demonstrate its authority and validity for this purpose; in other words, apply relevant critical standards to it.

Also look for material that contradicts your opinions to show that you are aware of, and have considered, arguments that are counter to your own. These counter arguments or evidence will help clarify and sharpen your own ideas and help you demonstrate why they are more convincing. Their use is a good guiding critical principle. If you are applying theory or research to practice, we have already shown in Chapter 2 how you can use the literature more directly by critically examining how and why you adapted an idea for your own use, i.e. evaluate its purpose and usefulness.

To achieve an appropriate academic style you must view all knowledge as contextual (Baxter Magolda, 1992) – i.e. there are no right or wrong answers but the knowledge or evidence supporting opinions and views can be constructed, understood, and appraised in relation to a particular context or situation. As we have said, there is no absolute 'truth' and your tutor will be assessing your ability to gain an overview of the subject and support a particular position within it.

We can refer back to our viewpoint example and show some reasons for it.

Example

Assignment for a specialist area of social work: enabling others

Stage 1: My viewpoint

Good communication is essential when planning successfully for a placement student.

Stage 2: The reasons why I believe good communication is essential

1. *Interpersonal skills (good listening) helped me start the relationship with the student well – empathy, trust being built. Literature on interpersonal communication says these skills are crucial in forming relationships and for education. Dangers to be aware of are becoming too informal and friendly...*

2. *Better forming of communication lines with the university tutor would have enabled better understanding of their role and the ways I needed to liaise with them. I felt intimidated and assumed the tutor would not be available; bureaucracy issues were apparent. Literature on placements says this is a difficult area – need to be proactive. I can discuss ways I could do this better next time...*

3. *Liaison with my team beforehand helped the induction go smoothly – people on side, better prepared. Literature on team co-ordination for a project says that early contact allows problems to surface and be dealt before start. Literature on placement planning says early contact is essential but to also keep overall control by forming clear learning objectives for the student. Discuss links...*

ACTIVITY 5.1

If such a structure is useful to you, start to develop one for an assignment of your own. Our example was very linear in structure but you can do it using any method you like.

Stage 3: Developing points for each reason will make up the paragraphs

Once you have your reasons and the literature behind them, you can then break down each of your reasons into its main points or issues. Paragraphs then raise and develop these particular issues or points using appropriate evidence. Remember the idea is to try and persuade the reader. Often the first sentence is the key point itself – i.e. it explains what the paragraph is about and contains the main idea. This 'topic sentence' need not come first in the paragraph but it has to be somewhere because it asserts and controls the paragraph's main idea. You can place it in the middle if you have information that needs to precede it. You can put it at the end if you want your reader to consider your line of reasoning before you declare your main point.

However you do it, the line of reasoning and its evidence should follow and be linked logically within these paragraphs. As you develop the point you tell the reader where you are going with it, by making use of the literature, linking back to the reason and the main argument as appropriate. Ideally it is best to sort out one point before moving onto another but if you do need to stop and then return to a point later, make sure you tell the reader what you're doing and why.

The next point should always be introduced. Using linking words or 'signposts' helps the reader make the transition from one paragraph or point to the next. There are different ways to do this depending on the way you want to develop your argument.

Here are some examples.

- Contrast, or taking a sudden turn in reasoning – *but...*, *however...*, *on the other hand...*, *although...*, *and yet...*
- Cause and effect – *therefore...*, *as a result of...*, *for this reason...*, *consequently...*
- Sequence – *following...*, *before... first...*, *finally...*,
- Illustration – *for example...*, *for instance...*, *such as...*, *in this case...*
- Add weight – *similarly...*, *in addition...*, *moreover...*
- Conclusion – *In conclusion...*, *accordingly...*, *to sum up...*;

Returning to our example, we can see a specific point being developed for the first reason.

Example

Assignment for a specialist area of social work: enabling others

Stage 1: My viewpoint
Good communication is essential when planning successfully for a placement student.

Stage 2: First reason
1. Interpersonal skills (good listening) helped me start the relationship with the student well – empathy, trust being built.

Stage 3: Particular point/issue to develop for this reason
This is the point (topic sentence) *Listening to the student rather than talking at her made our initial meeting a very positive one.*

Define *Listening entails...*

> **Develop – how and why** *Letting the student speak first not only allowed me an understanding of her unique situation and needs, it also made her feel at ease with me and to start to trust me...*
>
> **Link to reason/argument** *Understanding her needs and circumstances informed my planning...; but this conversation also formed a bond between us...*
>
> **Evidence/connections** *Bloggs (2003) explains how listening is more important than talking because it shows respect to others...and she responded by... Adult learning theory similarly emphasises the need for respect for learners...*
>
> **Link to next point/paragraph** *However, the relationship still needs to remain professional...*

Once your main text is structured you will need an introduction and a conclusion.

Introductions

We want to emphasise the crucial importance of the introduction. This is probably the most important part of your work in terms of ensuring your writing keeps to task. Don't attempt it until you have a good grip on your argument, reasons and points.

- Set the overall context but also state the main issues you are going to write and why, it will help you focus and places your argument into a wider picture.
- Point out the limitations and what you are not going to consider.
- Introduce the structure and sequence of your work.

Conclusions

A conclusion is all too often just a paragraph stuck on the end of the piece of work, which either summarises what has come before or gives the result of what happened.

A conclusion offers the chance to do much more than this. It can deliver a concise consideration of the overall meaning you have gained from critical thinking and reflection on your practice and/or learning. That is, it can sum up the major issues and points raised from your evaluation of the outcomes and consequences; plus what they may, or will, mean for social work, for your practice or for yourself.

ACTIVITY **5.2**

Try writing a brief introduction or conclusion for our example assignment.

Critical style

Developing an appropriate critical style does take time and practice, especially when initial thoughts tend to be very descriptive – here are some more tips. Table 5.3 below (Cottrell, 2003, p232) shows how the more normal, descriptive way of writing can be developed into a critical academic style by listing how each element should be enhanced – again we can see similar methods of questioning, delving deeper, assessing and judging things as we do in critical-thinking abilities.

Table 5.3 Descriptive to critical writing (Cottrell, 2003)

Descriptive writing	Critical analytic writing
States what happened	Identifies the significance
States what something is like	Evaluates (judges the value of) strengths and weaknesses
Gives the story so far	Weighs one piece of information against another
States the order in which things happened	Makes reasoned judgements
Says how to do something	Argues a case according to the evidence
Explains what a theory says	Shows why something is relevant or suitable
Explains how something works	Indicates why something will work (best)
Notes the method used	Indicates whether something is appropriate or suitable
Says when something occurred	Identifies why the timing is of importance
States the different components	Weighs up the importance of component parts
States options	Gives reasons for selecting each option
Lists details	Evaluates the relative significance of details
Lists in any order	Structures information in order of importance
States links between items	Shows the relevance of links between pieces of information
Gives information	Draws conclusions

Academic style – some hints for vocabulary and grammar

Try more formal, specific words, e.g.:

- *Examine* instead of *look at;*
- *Has the potential* instead of *might;*
- *Enables* instead of *makes it possible.*

Try the passive voice in places:

- *Assessments are started by gathering relevant information* instead of *you start assessments by gathering relevant information.*

Use more cautious language to avoid sweeping statements:

- *The introduction of the new policy could be seen as…*

Use noun phrases which cut down the use of words, especially verbs for a more succinct text:

- *Carer's rights* instead of *The rights of the carer;*
- *Recently issued policies* instead of *Policies that have been issued recently;*
- *The effectiveness of the courses made them very popular* instead of *The treatments were effective and this made them very popular.*

Using the literature

As you probably realise, your success very much depends on the type of literature you read (its relevancy and authority) and your understanding of it, not how much you read – quality not quantity. As a practitioner you will also be using contextual information such as legislation, case law, policy and practice guidance documents, as well as theory and research. Your tutor, your reading lists and handouts will direct you to relevant and authoritative literature and you will be looking up more references for any specialist areas, using print and electronic resources. The particular problem areas associated with using literature are detailed below.

Making unsubstantiated comments

The biggest single piece of advice given back to students is: *Do not make unsubstantiated comments, or sweeping generalisations.* In other words, provide the evidence to support your point. This does not mean you never give your point of view, it just means there should be something or someone else to back you up. Here's an example:

> In my experience I have seen how more effective accounting procedures allow direct allocations of limited funds, and enable targeted services to improve. Jones (2004) also shows how services can benefit when enhanced management systems are put in place, especially with reduced resources, even though Smith (2003) had earlier argued that services always became worse after cutbacks. The process of selecting targeted services enabled us to develop our priorities with the service users more positively...

Avoiding plagiarism

If you do not say where your evidence or your ideas have come from you will be making claims to knowledge that is not yours (which is plagiarism). Therefore references to evidence in the literature should appear whenever you are mentioning another's ideas, theory, material, or research, whether you are directly quoting or paraphrasing them. This has to follow certain academic 'rules' in order to be valid and you should follow the appropriate system as advocated by your academic institution. Bournemouth University uses the Harvard system of referencing. This can be seen in our examples below, and the Appendix provides further advice.

You can use someone else's work in three main ways:

1. You can mention their theory or idea:

   The process used incorporated some of the elements of task-centred work (Coulshed, 1991) and systems approach (Payne, 1991; Milner and O'Byrne, 1998) because the...

2. You can summarise in your own words what someone else has written, either small sections or overall views:

   Mrs Jones felt helpless and frustrated at her inability to improve her daughter's situation and appeared to get many colds and coughs during this time, which weakened her ability to look after her. Research has shown that those who experience life events that are seen as uncontrollable are more likely to become ill (Stern et al., 2003, cited in Gross, 2004).

3. You can repeat a small section of what someone has written and place it in quotation marks, or indent it:

   It is not sufficient to be reflective; we also need to use new understandings in our future actions. As Adams et al. (2002, p87) point out: 'reflection on its own views the situation unchanged, whereas critical practice is capable of change'.

Try this method of remembering how to present other people's evidence: Ask – *Says who*? and *So what*? In other words, say who says this – the opinion and the reference to who said it; and then state why you are telling the reader this – what is your point here? Often we read assignments and case studies and ask ourselves: what is the point of the writer telling us that, it just appears to be packaging? Always ask yourself: what am I trying to say and why? It will help you to be more focused.

Paraphrasing others – some pointers

- Express the person's main ideas in your own words.
- Keep it simple and concise.
- Don't use the same sentence structure.

Whichever way you use the work of other people, you *must* cite where the work came from in the text itself and provide a reference to the complete work in either a reference list or a bibliography at the end of your work. In the Harvard system of referencing the citation in the text uses the author's last name and year, and the references list or bibliography will be in alphabetical order by author's last name. It is important to look up the rules for your particular institution and become familiar with them. See the appendix for further help on the Harvard style of referencing.

Effective reading

It does take time and practice to develop your reading in order to locate relevant and useful material. Here are a few initial ideas to help you start.

- Use the guidance provided by your educational institution on gaining access to and using the most relevant electronic databases and printed materials. Use the librarians for advice too. You don't want to waste time at this end of the process.
- Reading the literature while you are developing your viewpoint should encompass the wider topic area. Reading when you know your viewpoint will enable you to focus and

identify the more relevant pieces of text easily and save your time. Make a note of particular quotes (keep them as short as possible) or paraphrase ideas (summarise in your own words). Also note the complete reference to the book, journal, etc., at the time.

- Next, write down a brief explanation of what this means to you – what do you understand it to mean – do you agree or disagree with it – why? This becomes easier if you are applying what you read into practice straight away, or you have opportunities for discussion about the literature with your peers.

- As we have seen, as you start writing the first draft of your assignment, you will have a good idea of what you are trying to say so that when you refer back to these notes you can choose those that are applicable to what you are talking about and integrate them.

Using 'I'

N.B. You must check your institution's own rules on this – some universities do not allow the use of the first person in written assignments.

Using the first-person 'I' is appropriate for academic reflective writing and for developing personal and professional qualities of self-awareness, reflection, analysis and critique (Hamill, 1999). However, this does not mean the writing should be emotional or subjective (i.e. seen from your viewpoint only). Students who lack experience in writing and who start to use 'I' tend to be too descriptive in their style – e.g. *I did this... I did that....* So 'I' has to be used carefully and much care has to be taken to avoid informal or conversational tones within a reflective assignment.

Using 'I' should encourage a confident stance, i.e. directness in saying what you mean and the message you are trying to get across. With the addition of the literature, and your viewpoint and reasons, it creates an appropriate academic style.

Here is a short general example from social work to show how it can all come together using the Harvard system of referencing (from Watson et al., 2002, p128):

> *I would argue that it is how we as social workers use our legal power in practice that is the crux of developing partnership. That we have legal power does not absolve us of our professional duty to our clients. Jenny and her family members had a right to be treated with respect, openness and honesty (Banks, 1995) in my interventions with them. To me, this included acknowledging to them the impact on their lives that my legal power to intervene to safeguard and promote Jenny's welfare was having. Research indicates that family members stressed the importance of being cared about as people (Thoburn, Lewis, and Shemmings, 1995). This extended to identifying and acknowledging areas of Mr Jones's care where he was safeguarding and promoting Jenny's welfare. As Morrison (1996, p136) suggests: 'Partnership is about working with parents and their networks to enable them to carry out the responsibility shared by both the state and parents to promote the welfare of children.'*

Finishing writing

Check coverage and relevancy – match what you say you will focus on in the introduction against what you have written about in the main body and the conclusion. Also, refer back to your original list of what the assignment has to cover – make sure you have covered all that is asked of you. Ask yourself – where have I shown this?

Think critically about your work before handing it in. Evaluate it using the guidance given here or even try marking it using your institution's assessment criteria.

Review

As we have seen, writing is a process. Each draft will enable you to show areas of learning and development in more structured, explicit and academic ways as you build up a better understanding of what you have done. The main difficulty with writing is to get the real meaning of what you are trying to say past the code of language in which you have to say it.

Each rewrite should allow this by giving you the opportunity to:

- think about and analyse what you want to say more thoroughly;
- reflect on what you have achieved or learnt more deeply;
- read more around the issues and increase your ability to express your understanding of the links to the literature.

By enabling a clear and deeper understanding of learning and practice development, the processes of writing should enhance critical practice, which is itself a process of self-inquiry and, at times, transformative change. Our next chapter looks at these ideas more closely.

FURTHER READING

Cottrell, S (2003) *The study skills handbook*. London: Palgrave Macmillan.

Watson, F Burrows, H and Player, C (2002) *Integrating theory and practice in social work education*. London: Jessica Kingsley.

Chapter 6
Developing critical practice

ACHIEVING POST QUALIFYING SOCIAL WORK AWARDS

This chapter will help you to meet the following National Occupational Standards for Social Work.

- Key role 5: Unit 14: Manage and be accountable for your own work
- Key role 6: Unit 19: Work within agreed standards of social work practice and ensure own professional development
- Key role 6: Unit 20: Mange complex ethical issues, dilemmas and conflicts.

If you are a registered social worker, this chapter will also assist you to evidence post-registration training and learning. It relates to the national post-qualifying framework for social work education and training in particular the national criteria at the specialist level:

(ii) Think critically about their own practice in the context of the GSCC *Codes of Practice*, national and international codes of professional ethics and the principles of diversity, equality and social inclusion in a wide range of situations, including those associated with inter-agency and inter-professional work.

(iii) Consolidate and consistently demonstrate in direct work with users of social care services and/or carers the full range of social work competences across all units of the National Occupational Standards for Social Work and in the context of one area of specialist social work practice.

(vii) Work effectively in a context of risk, uncertainty conflict and contradiction.

Our aim in this chapter is to focus on more critical approaches to practice rather than particular methods and techniques. Everyday social work obviously deals with risk, complexity and contingency, and so:

- there will be range of 'solutions';

- things will change;

- outcomes cannot be predicted with utter certainty;

- certain values and assumptions may not be valid in the future;

- there will be many other perspectives on a situation.

Working with uncertainty, by allowing for contingency and checking up on how things are going, is more likely to lessen its threat and its ability to make us feel defensive. We need practices that allow us to accept and deal with ever-changing situations creatively, rather than practices that make us follow prescriptions. It is, therefore, useful to consider critical thinking for practice within its widest and most holistic sense as being critical or taking a critical stance, and this involves practitioners' overall approach to their work.

To do this we will explore how practitioners develop their expertise using knowledge and experience in order to create their own practice theory, but also gain the understandings and open mindset necessary to approach the uncertainty of practice in a positive way. We then look pragmatically at where criticality fits within these ways of working.

First, we can examine how practice is developed over time. Many of these ideas are based on Fook et al.'s (2000) research on the development of expertise.

New practice

Once qualified, or indeed when taking up any new post or starting a placement, a practitioner's professional development and learning start to centre on a range of work-related aspects and knowledge.

> *The most obvious relates to a particular workplace setting or activity system and is bound up with the systems' rules, tools, norms, objectives, divisions of labour and communities of practice.*
> (Knight, 2006, p32).

Beginning to deal with this type of 'how to' knowledge is where a practitioner's ignorance becomes obvious and can cause anxiety. It may well be the reason why many new qualified workers take a very prescriptive, rule-based approach to try to ensure they don't do anything wrong. In many ways such a focus on detail and correctness ensures that practitioners can be more critically aware of what they are doing than experienced workers who have established routines.

The key for workers in these situations is to attain a balance between the need for certainty and the need to be aware of other ways of doing, or thinking about, practice. Here is where critical reflection (especially involving others) can play a key role in developing confidence through the analysis of strengths-based practice, but also allow consideration of alternative options, viewpoints, etc., within a safe space, and ensure that a blinkered and uncritical rigidity does not get established.

Good critical thinking should evolve alongside a person's development within their practice. However, there is an important issue to take account of. The aim of many critical methods is to create doubt and critique of ongoing actions. We therefore cannot undertake them as a set of explicit and separate exercises because it is not possible to act confidently and thoughtfully while doubting oneself at the same time (Van Manen, 1999). We can, however, adopt critical practice more as an acceptable way of 'being' by undertaking tasks in positive and confident, but also open and flexible, ways. To achieve this it is necessary to embed criticality as approaches within professional and experienced practice itself, rather than use critical methods as remedial, 'bolt-ons' which are more likely to suffer when workloads rise.

We look first at the dangers of developing in practice uncritically.

The dangers of more experience

On a day-to-day level there are dangers associated with the development of experience in practice. Any practice can easily fall into purely intuitive and routine methods that are followed because they are safer and less time-consuming. We develop rules of thumb and standardise our approaches to problems in order to survive our workloads. However, these habitual practices are more difficult to keep under critical control, and they tend not to adapt to new circumstances easily.

In these situations uncertain problems may be 'pretended' to be certain so we can accommodate them into existing practices or our value systems. Or they are simplified by ignoring certain difficult aspects. Matching similarities is easier than acknowledging dissimilarities because they confirm rather than deny our generalisations and so fit our existing knowledge. As human beings we tend to give more credence to viewpoints that are close to our own, and tend to devalue or reject information that conflicts with our beliefs. This saves time and energy and makes us feel less threatened because knowledge relies for its verification on belief; but eventually the process of evaluating our work becomes lost.

As we become less subject to dissimilarity and surprise, our experiences become non-learning situations, as we don't notice what is actually happening. So even though we have more experience in a particular environment we do not automatically acquire more valid knowledge.

In this respect, the main benefits that our post-qualifying students report when undertaking our programmes are that they:

- provide reassurance of good practices already being undertaken via discussion with others and use of the literature; but also
- enable them to stop, think and reassess their practices, which allows them to see where they have fallen into pure routine and adopt more appropriate methods and approaches.

Learning new knowledge, talking to others, sharing ideas, applying and connecting them to practice, and then reflecting on what happens, engage the brain in a different mode. Post-qualifying and other continuing professional development programmes can encourage better-quality approaches through the content of the curriculum and its assessment, and allow the opportunity and encouragement to undertake more critical work practices.

Embedding criticality

If we look at a more positive model of expertise we can see how the holistic notion of professionally developed practice requires a critical overall disposition or stance, and also where critical thinking can be embedded as approaches to enhance existing practice.

Research adapted from Cust (1995, cited in Macaulay, 2001) shows how experienced practitioners (or 'experts' as they call them) encounter new situations. They:

- are in control of their thinking, are i.e. aware of, understand, self-direct and self-evaluate it throughout;
- have clusters of 'tacit knowledge' which form 'patterns' and represent the learning and generalising from previous experiences, from research and theory;
- recognise other meaningful patterns and principles, and irrelevant aspects, in a situation and link to these existing known patterns;
- and so gain an intuitive grasp of it;
- while assessing it in depth;
- in order to select 'schema' (patterns or outlines formed in the mind);
- which when adapted to the problem;
- is likely to effectively represent it as well as suggesting solution procedures;
- but will periodically check to review and progress and evaluate outcomes.

Such 'experts' are seen to focus initially on the holistic assessment of a situation, rather than on explicit reasoning and analysis. In other words, they have established the necessary intuitive links to bring the different parts of a situation into a meaningful whole, to allow it to make sense for them. Each situation they face may be different but they will recognise enough of the parts to make general sense of the whole, in order to start to deal with it. Schön (1983) explained this by stating that experienced practitioners know how to define the nature of the problem or situation first – they can more easily *name and frame* a situation.

ACTIVITY **6.1**

Start to link the use of our critical resources (knowledge, critical concepts, standards, strategies, or habits of mind) to the various elements of 'expert' practice seen above.

Embedding critical thinking and developing holistic critical approaches:

If we now list the key expert practice areas gathered from the ideas above we can begin to see where relevant critical thinking activities can be most appropriately and positively embedded. See Table 6.1.

Table 6.1 Elements and activities of critical 'expert' practice

Experience	Critical thinking activities
1. Awareness, control and evaluation of thinking processes	Thinking about thinking (meta-thinking) Recognising and questioning arguments, etc. Identifying and challenging own and others' assumptions.
2. Developing clusters of knowledge	Keeping up to date; reading the literature. Integrating values and experience. Holding views based on valid experiential evidence but seeking and accepting relevant but alternative viewpoints and perspectives Creating and evaluating practice theory.
3. Assessment of situations in depth 'naming and 'framing' Selection and adaptation of 'schema' or framework that fits	Understanding alternative perspective/s or reframing a situation. Understanding when more information and input is required, knowing where and how to get it. Lateral/creative/flexible thinking; problem-solving.
4. Decisions leading to action	Decision-making and planning; use of discretion; responsibility; risk assessment Seeking out and taking proper account of all stakeholders' input Thinking through implications Predicting possible outcomes, allowing for alternatives
5. Monitoring progress and evaluating outcomes. Adapting and changing where necessary. Ongoing learning	Formulating clear aims/objectives at start, getting feedback and making judgements. Using feedback and evaluation from all concerned parties, especially people who use services. Making informal learning more explicit. Embedding formal learning. Sharing and developing learning within the organisation.

As we can see, there are many critical-thinking activities that can be aligned and embedded with the areas of expert practice to allow the best possible (i.e. most critical) approaches. However, it is not just about 'bolting on' a set of separate standards, strategies or methods to existing practice (although these may be important at various points). The notion of true critical practice becomes established with inherent approaches to various work practices and with holistic habits of mind – i.e. critical 'being'. For example, decisions would not just be retrospectively appraised according to a tick-box set of criteria in order to be justified; rather the process of decision-making would be undertaken with the implicit aim of identifying relevant but alternative decisions right at the start. Similarly, problem-solving would start with questioning the problem itself and gaining different viewpoints on it.

Fook et al. (2000) take this idea further. They show that practice at an expert level is not just about more knowledge and understanding from experience, but about dimensions such as creativity, artistry, openness to new ideas and also about framing situations in complex rather than routine ways. These dimensions are associated with a process approach to practice that is committed to engaging in a particular way, rather than committed to particular or expected outcomes. A true 'expert' thus approaches any situation as a potentially unpredictable and changeable one by naturally identifying its multifaceted aspects and considering a range of options to name and frame it.

The naming and framing of situations is one major area where more critical thinking can be triggered automatically, usually by recognition of something not 'normal' – possibly an unexpected action or outcome, or an intuitive feeling of unease. This is where a critical practitioner acknowledges the difference to a usual pattern rather than ignoring it, pretending it is ok, or standardising it. It is where the benefits of keeping up to date in a professional area of practice and having the necessary critical resources come to the fore. Such a practitioner will have more knowledge and awareness to recognise the incident for what it is, and more self-confidence to deal with it explicitly. The outcomes from such creative and innovative practice can result in transformative development of expertise.

This type of professional development is, therefore, not necessarily dependent on length of experience but rather on a particular disposition and mindset. Also, in this respect, we could say that such 'expertise' cannot be defined in prescriptive, narrow terms.

Evidenced-informed practice

There is a large amount of debate concerning evidence-informed or evidence-based practice and its place within social work. It is not within the remit of this handbook to explore the arguments further and we have already looked at the critical use of literature for our purposes. As students within an academic environment you will be expected to gain an understanding of the current theory, research focus and policy development within your post-qualifying specialism and discuss such issues in your assignments. As professionals we have already seen that new knowledge and ideas enhance and develop practice expertise, but your depth of involvement with different types of research material will depend on various issues, for example:

- the emphasis of your work within a medical model (which is highly evidence-based);
- the research culture of your organisation.

To sum up, we could say that to apply or base practice on any type of evidence without moral or ethical sensitivity, or a wider assessment of context, individual circumstances, situational requirements, or risk assessment of possible implications would be deemed 'uncritical' practice and is unacceptable.

Review

We do not have to pretend we are in a perfect world and always able to do the right thing. What we need to show and evidence is how we take account of the uncertainty and complexity of our role and how we try to work from a critical stance. Thinking critically must not be about feeling threatened or being made to feel inadequate. It is an holistic, open and positive way of approaching the world, and a natural one:

In as far as 'critical skills' go, learn to notice hunches, intuitions, gut feelings, the 'critique' is 'in there'.
(Stokoe, 2003)

An awareness and acceptance of uncertainty in the practice of any professional is an important way to lessen stress. There are no perfect solutions out there to find, so we cannot be called on to work perfectly. If we accept the fact that the things we do or decide on are still dependent on something uncertain or on future happenings, and work in a way that takes account of that (i.e. constantly reviewing the things we deal with, decide on, or do), then this is really what 'thinking critically' is all about.

As Taylor and White (2006) show, critical practice is not about *being certain* (the *certain* thing is not necessarily the *right* thing) – it is about being able to deal with uncertainty using sound, valid and accountable processes and, where appropriate, maintaining a position of *respectful uncertainty*, or at least holding onto doubt for longer and seeking out other possible versions.

How this stance can be used and developed within continuing learning and facilitated and enabled in others is the subject of the next chapter.

FURTHER READING

Adams, R, Dominelli, L and Payne, M (eds) (2002) *Critical practice in social work*. Basingstoke: Palgrave.

O'Sullivan, T (1999) *Decision making in social work*. London: Macmillan.

Chapter 7
Continuing learning – a critical approach

We have explored where criticality fits within established ways of working to foster more critical practice. Now we can look at how it can be developed for ourselves, and enabled for others, within continuing learning experiences.

Ongoing work-based or practice learning can occur in many different ways (from taking part in planned, formal courses, through to informal and unplanned day-to-day encounters) and can involve our colleagues and sometimes our managers.

We will look firstly at maximising learning from all work-based learning situations, secondly at enabling criticality in others, and finally at social learning cultures. Some of these ideas have been drawn from and are explored further in our text on *Enabling and assessing work-based learning for social work* (Williams and Rutter, 2007).

Maximising ongoing learning

The type of ongoing learning required to develop skills, abilities and attributes in the workplace is multi-layered. There is no single theory of learning in the workplace and, in fact, Cheetham and Chivers (2001) point out the dangers of placing too much reliance on a single approach, and argue for seeking to provide exposure to as wide a variety of learning mechanisms as possible. They encourage practitioners to view all experiences as potential learning experiences. In particular, they advocate a mindset of continuing learning from the outset in practice and collaboration with others in learning.

In this respect, practitioners who already have the skills, abilities and attributes of self-directed learners should be able to make the most of the learning potential found within work situations. Those who are lucky enough to work in a positive learning culture that encourages sharing of knowledge, plus feedback and evaluation of services, should be able to truly maximise this potential for themselves and others.

The skills of self-directed (also referred to as *autonomous* or *independent*) learning allow practitioners to:

- take the initiative in diagnosing their learning needs;
- create their own learning objectives;
- identify, locate and evaluate the resources needed;
- choose and implement appropriate learning strategies;
- evaluate learning outcomes.

These are useful skills, but, as with any process, a more holistic and critical stance can foster a deeper and more meaningful engagement. For example, here it could encourage a practitioner to actively seek and reflect on more critical feedback from service users or colleagues and gain another perspective.

Also, recognising the need to make the most of informal, as well as more formal learning events, to enable change and flexibility in self and practice thus becomes a more critical habit of mind. Informal learning covers events like observation, feedback, dialogue and co-working, and usually results in new knowing or understanding that is either tacit or regarded as part of a person's general capability, rather than as something learnt. However, it is a key area for professional development. For example, Becher (1999) reports that professionals learn six times as much through non-formal as through formal means.

To make developmental informal learning more explicit requires a commitment to recording, reflecting on and using ideas, challenges, etc. We can particularly see how our critical reflection model (Chapter 4) could help to lift subconscious learning up to a more conscious and formalised level, using the analytical (*how?* and *why?*) and evaluative (*how well?*) stages. Only such conscious learning becomes educative in a true sense (i.e. meaningful and owned), and thus able to impact on practice. Being aware of and deliberating with informal learning can create and consolidate new and improved understanding. This developed understanding for practice can then be used explicitly for more formal situations. The consolidation unit within the PQ specialist awards particularly requires such developmental practice understanding.

We need to repeat the major proviso that reflecting alone can become self-justifying or self-pitying, and so anyone reflecting should have input and support from others to help them gain different, more balanced and more critical perspectives. Reflection benefits greatly by becoming a social learning process, as we shall see below.

Enabling others

Professional development is obviously a complex form of growth that is more than the sum of its individual parts and is never complete. A key point is that, as professionals, we will not automatically continue to learn and develop simply because we have gained more experience, or have reflected on it. As mentioned earlier, increasing experience may have a detrimental effect on learning as the associated increase in confidence can at times lead us into uncritical routine, where we make assumptions and fail to notice the small but possibly crucial differences between one situation and another.

Therefore, the support and facilitation of professional development becomes an important issue. In the world of social work the need for practice education is now being placed within all PQ specialist roles and there is an expectation that, from the point of qualification, all social workers will begin to take some responsibility for supporting the learning of others (GSCC, 2005). On qualification, social workers need to be able to work interprofessionally in a wide variety of complex settings and be evidence-informed. They need to be critically reflective practitioners who are self-aware, critically analysing, evaluating, reviewing and updating their values, skills and knowledge, practising flexibly and reflexively, exploring alternative approaches and being open to change in all contexts.

Qualified practitioners, therefore, need to focus on more than just 'teaching' specific practice skills, and to enable all levels of learners to also develop the kind of stance required for such critical and flexible practice. This will ensure that, as learners and as qualified workers, they will be able to adapt, develop and fine-tune their approach to practice in a way which is tailored to meet individual needs, aligned to our notion of expertise as shown earlier. Many authors show how this support should incorporate elements which not only allow planning, reflection, articulation and recording of 'events' but also take account of an individual's approach and attitude to their practice, encouraging them to take responsibility for that practice through a critical questioning stance (e.g. McGill and Beaty, 1995; Moon, 1999b).

ACTIVITY 7.1

List some methods which you, as a qualified practitioner, might use to adopt such a critical questioning stance in order to take account of an individual learner's approach and attitude to their practice, and encourage them to take responsibility for that practice.

What differences would there be in your approach and methods between working with a qualifying student and an experienced member of staff?

Appropriate methods

Dialogue is a key essential element in learning, and discussion can happen in many work-based scenarios, e.g. supervision, mentoring, workshops. Remember, there are no 'right' questions to ask learners because there are no clear-cut answers – 'certain' reasons and justifications are not always appropriate when talking about professional knowledge. In fact, as with any conversational situation, it is also about listening correctly (i.e. actively, without interruption or judgement) and about reflecting back what you think you've heard for clarification. McGill and Beaty (1995) recommend the use of questions that are open (e.g. *how...? ...why?*), affective (e.g. *how are you feeling?*) and probing/checking (e.g. *when...? where...? in what way...?*).

Critical questioning (Brookfield, 1987) takes the dialogue process one step further in drawing out not only assumptions and underlying thoughts but also personal givens and accepted public truths. We are all imprisoned in our *own histories and constrained by the inevitable narrow paradigms of thought and action we inhabit* (Brookfield, 1987, p91). Questioning someone to elicit self-scrutiny of such issues must obviously not become, or be seen as, behaviour that insults, threatens or attacks their self-esteem. It is not what you do but how the learner perceives that action, which will lead to their response. If the learner perceives questioning as threatening in any way (whether you think it is or not), they may retreat or attack, and the learning experience will become a very negative situation.

Critical questioning, therefore, involves very skilful framing of insightful and empathetic questions to encourage analysis and challenge thinking. This is a skill that may need training and subsequent refinement for qualified practitioners enabling others, but many skills may be transferred from the type of work undertaken already with service users. Brookfield (1987, pp93–4) suggests the following general guidelines.

- Be specific – relate questions to particular events, situations, people and actions.
- Work from the particular to the general – exploring a general theme within the context of a specific event helps people feel they are in familiar territory.
- Be conversational – informal, non-threatening tones help people feel comfortable.

We would add another suggestion – be aware of the effect your questioning is having and watch for any negative signs, e.g. non-response, a defensive position being argued too aggressively, brooding resignation.

Enabling critical refection and practice

Facilitating the critical reflection of others is obviously a difficult balance between providing a safe but appropriately challenging learning situation. As the aim of critical reflection is to create at least some doubt and critique of ongoing actions, the whole process can be extremely anxiety-provoking, especially if a learner is unsure and lacks confidence in the first place. There is another issue to consider, which relates to criticality. Although many competency-type skills may be easily reflected on and self-appraised, a person's disposition at work and the approaches they take to work situations will be so closely tied in with their personality and previous history that for many a truly honest examination is very difficult to achieve. The requirement for critically and honestly appraising one's own assumptions, deliberations, decisions or actions requires a particular humility alongside a confident allowance of uncertainty. Obviously this is a very complex notion, especially in the early stages of a career when a worker is setting out to prove themselves. The need for such honesty and humility especially holds true for the qualified practitioner if they are truly working in a partnership of trust with a learner, i.e. they have to model this behaviour in order to be credible.

If you have successfully enabled a learner to critically reflect, then ensuring there are effective learning outputs from the process is the next step. The qualified practitioner should help the learner to scaffold and integrate the knowledge and understanding that result from critical reflection and place it into a work-based context for future use, i.e. covering knowledge, skills and values (knowing, acting and being) for practice itself. This could involve further questioning or designing learning activities, such as use of other critical incidents, imagined scenarios or role play.

ACTIVITY **7.2**

It can be rather oppressive to insist on learners following specific and prescriptive instructions to 'make' them reflect.

Research various models of facilitating reflection and note their common aspects. Develop your own model incorporating the features you think are most important. How can you encourage a learner to develop their own model which is specific to their needs?

To take a wider view on enabling the critical practice of others, we can return to Taylor and White's (2006) idea that critical practice is about being able to deal with uncertainty using sound, valid and accountable processes and, where appropriate, maintaining a position of 'respectful uncertainty'. Gray and Gibbons (2007, p235) advocate that good prudent judgement is an individual virtue that must be cultivated beyond the use of structured, linear decision-making frameworks which tend to develop *the false assumption that the procedures or codes or framework will resolve the ethical problem when, clearly, there are no answers, only choices, and often the right choices make waves'.*

Here, a qualified practitioner can help any learner to at least hold onto doubt for longer and seek out other possible versions as they suggest. However, being adaptable enough to act in a flexible manner in a wide range of circumstances is a difficult call and there may be many other methods which help foster a more open approach. What may be needed overall is the opportunity (with appropriate space and freedom, i.e. no risk) to explore alternative approaches and choices wherever possible. This may help reinforce understanding that there is usually more than one possible interpretation or approach to a complex situation, and that there is often no 'right answer' or 'right way' to do something in professional practice.

We could say that enabling others to practise more critically and reflectively exposes us all to different ways of representing what we do. So the best type of work-based learning can help all participants to see their processes of reasoning and judgement more realistically and to become more reflexive, analytic and systematic in their sense-making activities (Taylor and White, 2006, p950). In other words, we may all learn from this involvement in learning, as the relative importance of learning from experience becomes greater the more expert we become. Perhaps this is a way to build true communities of practice which reject the separation of training and learning from practice (Lave and Wenger, 1991) and enable the organisation to learn as well. We will briefly look at this as our next area of focus.

Social learning cultures

There is a growing recognition of the central importance of organisations having a culture that supports continuous learning and enables the conversion of individual learning to organisational change. We have already mentioned that the system we work in, and the people we work with, can affect our opportunities and ability to learn. Here we can look at social and environmental factors for learning effectively. Knight et al. (2006) advocate spaces for the creation of shared meaning, e.g. for collegiality and participation; and for processes such as reflection to capture, codify but also share implicit knowledge. The authors describe professional development as the development of capabilities that actually occur as a consequence of situated social practices and the work-based learning environment.

The idea of ongoing and more critical learning, therefore, needs to an embedded part of being a professional social worker (as it should with any profession) and this means employers playing their full role in developing appropriate cultures and opportunities for it. Nixon and Murr (2006, p802) take the social/group learning issue further into an analysis of the role of the organisation, and show that the organisational context is itself critical to the development of practice learning. They highlight how informal learning is tied up with communities of practice that can supply the social learning opportunities, and argue that practice learning makes a contribution to the quality of professional practice and the organisation's services too. Learning, therefore, does not just remain with the individual; it needs to transfer in order to create the changes necessary in the organisation for improved performance.

As we have seen, the change in GSCC requirements for PQ specialist awards aims to ensure that more social workers develop basic skills in the facilitation of all forms of work-based learning and assessment. Although not enough in itself to bring about the development of learning organisations, this (and the requirements for post-registration training and learning – PRTL) could help support the development of appropriate 'micro' learning cultures, in which all staff both recognise and value the role that they have to play in supporting individual and organisational learning.

This is obviously a huge area for debate and may be an issue you want to discuss or explore further within your programme and/or workplace.

QUESTIONS

How can you deal with a negative work place learning culture?

Which areas of professionalism are likely to suffer?

List any ideas that may enable more collaborative learning in your workplace.

Practical ideas for developing a learning culture

- Learning sets, e.g. for post-qualifying study.
- Mentoring/coaching/induction schemes.

- Engaging with projects, action research.
- Staff development to encourage reflective as well as managerial supervision.

Review

We have tried in this chapter to develop an understanding of how critical practice and the notion of capability can be developed for ourselves, and enabled for others, within continuing learning experiences. As work-based learners we all need directed but risk-free opportunities to critically analyse and evaluate our practice, and explore alternative approaches wherever possible, in order to deal effectively with the continuing complexity of practice.

FURTHER READING

Beverley, A and Worsley, A (2007) *Learning and teaching in social work practice*. London: Palgrave Macmillan.

Gould, N and Baldwin, M (eds) (2004) *Social work, critical reflection and the learning organisation*. Aldershot: Ashgate

Williams, S and Rutter, L. (2007) *Enabling and assessing work-based learning for social work. Supporting the development of professional practice*. Birmingham: Learn to Care.

Chapter 8
Summary

As we have seen, our original set of intellectual resources for critical thinking can be applied to all areas of the PQ framework and be aligned with qualifying and post-qualifying activities such as critical reflection, reflective learning and critical writing. It comes down to three basic abilities – questioning, analysing, and evaluating – which dovetail into the various methods associated with professional practice as well as learning.

Critical reflection can enable the identification, exploration and understanding of practice activities – e.g. decision-making, managing risk, exercising power and responsibility, using discretion, integrating values. Reflective learning will enable these activities to develop with new knowledge and new experiences. Writing critically allows an appropriate academic structuring and evidencing of this reflection for assignments; and enables a more thorough critical analysis and evaluation of the knowledge and learning taking place.

This whole process can also constructively move our practice forward to incorporate any necessary change and development. In this way, practice knowledge is developed further for our selves, for others, and for the profession itself as we begin to develop and articulate our own practice theories, constantly evaluated in the light of new experience and knowledge. More holistically it develops a way of being as a practitioner.

We may not have a lot of time for critical thinking, reflection or writing, and as abilities or qualities they are processes that need experience and practice in order to be undertaken effectively. The PQ framework provides the opportunities for the experience and practice, and also gives you the credit for doing it. The other good news is that you can develop your abilities by understanding the various elements involved, and by having some methods to follow, adapt and make your own. In this respect we hope this handbook has given you a better understanding, as well as some useful ideas, to work with.

Finally, good thinking, reflecting and writing skills help you to deliver good social work, as you become more able to develop and articulate the resources and services for your service users, and be accountable for them. We hope that throughout all your efforts in developing critical thinking your service users will benefit.

References

Adams, R, Dominelli, L and Payne, M (eds) (2002) *Critical practice in social work.* Basingstoke: Palgrave.

Alter, C and **Egan, M** (1997) Logic modeling: A tool for teaching critical thinking in social work practice. *Journal of Social Work Education,* 33 (1), 85–103.

Argyris, C and SchÖn, D (1974) *Theory in practice: Increasing professional effectiveness.* San Francisco: Jossey Bass.

Bailin, S, Case, R, Coombs, JR and Daniels, LB (1999) Conceptualizing crtical thinking. *Journal of Curriculum Studies*, 31, 285–302.

Barnett, R (1997) *Higher education: A critical business.* Buckingham: Society for Research in Higher Education and Open University Press.

Baxter Magolda, M (1992) *Knowing and reasoning in college.* San Franciso: Jossey Bass.

Becher, Y (1999) *Professional practices: Commitment and capability in a changing environment.* New Brunswick, NJ: Transaction.

Bloom, BS jr (1956) *Taxonomy of educational objectives: Handbook 1. The cognitive domain.* New York: McKay.

Boud, D, Keogh, R and Walker, D (1985) *Reflection: Turning experience into learning.* London: Kogan Page.

Bowlby, J (1951) *Maternal care and mental health.* Report to the World Health Organisation. New York: Shocken Books.

Bowlby, J (1969) *Attachment and loss: Attachment.* New York: Basic Books.

Brockbank, A, and McGill, I (1998) *Facilitating reflective learning in higher education.* Buckingham: Society for Research into Higher Education and Open University Press.

Brookfield, S (1987) *Developing critical thinkers.* Milton Keynes: Open University Press.

Brown, RB and McCartney, S (2002) Multiple mirrors: Reflecting on reflections. In: R Adams, L Dominelli, and M Payne (eds) *Critical practice in social work*. London: Palgrave. pp16–31.

Burgess, RC (1999) Reflective practice: action learning sets for managers in social work. *Social Work Education,* 18 (3), 257–70.

Cheetham, G, and Chivers, G (2001) How professionals learn in practice: An investigation of informal learning amongst people working in professions. *Journal of European Industrial Training,* 25 (5), 248–92.

Coleman, H, Rogers, G and King, J (2002) Using portfolios to stimulate critical thinking in social work education. *Social Work Education,* 21 (5), 583–95.

Cottrell, S (2003) *The study skills handbook*. London: Palgrave Macmillan.

Curry, L and Wengin, JF (1993) *Educating the professional*. San Francisco: Jossey-Bass.

Eraut, M (1994) *Developing professional knowledge and competence*. London: Routledge.

Eraut, M (2003) The many meanings of theory and practice. *Learning in Health and Social Care*. 2 (4), 191–201.

Fisher, A (2001) *Critical thinking. An introduction.* Cambridge: Cambridge University.

Fisher, T and Somerton, J (2000) Reflection on action: The process of helping social workers to develop their use of theory in practice. *Social Work Education,* 19 (4), 387–401.

Fook, J, Ryan, M and Hawkins, L (2000) *Professional expertise: Practice, theory and education for working in uncertainty*. London: Whiting and Birch.

Ford, P, Johnston, B, Mitchell, R and Myles, F (2004) Social work education and criticality: some thoughts from research. *Social Work Education,* 23 (2), 185–98.

Ford, P, Johnston, B, Mitchell, R and Myles, F (2005) Practice learning and the development of students as critical practitioners: Some findings from research. *Social Work Education,* 24 (4), 391–407.

Ghaye, A and Ghaye, K (1998) *Teaching and learning through critical reflective practice.* London: David Fulton.

Gibbs, L and Gambrill, E (1999) *Critical thinking for social worker: Exercises for the helping profession.* London: Sage.

Gibbs, L and Gambrill, E (2002) *Evidence-based practice: Counter arguments to objections. Research on Social Work Practice*, 12 (3), 452–76.

Gould, N and Taylor, I (eds) (1996) *Reflective learning for social work*. London: Arena.

Gray, M and Gibbons, J (2007) There are no answers, only choices: Teaching ethical decision making in social work. *Australian Social Work,* (60) 2, 222–38.

GSCC (2005) *Post-qualifying framework for social work education and training*. London: GSCC.

Halonen, JS (1985) Demistifying critical thinking. *Teaching Psychology,* 22 (1), 75–81.

Hamill, C (1999) Academic essay writing in the first person: A guide for undergraduates. *Nursing Standard*, 13 (44), 38–40.

Ixer, G (1999) Theres no such thing as reflection. *British Journal of Social Work*, 29, 513–27.

Johns, C (2000) *Becoming a reflective practitioner*. Oxford: Blackwell.

Knight, P, Tait, J and Yorke, M (2006) The professional learning of teachers in higher education. *Studies in Higher Education,* 31 (3), 319–39.

Kolb, DA (1984) *Experiential learning. Experience as the source of learning and development.* New Jersey: Prentice Hall.

Lave, J and Wenger, E (1991) *Situated learning: Legitimate peripheral participation.* Cambridge: Cambridge University Press.

Macaulay, C (2000) Transfer of learning In: VE Cree and C Macaulay (eds) *Transfer of learning in professional and vocational learning.* London: Routledge, pp1–26.

Maslin-Prothero, S (ed) (2001) *Bailliere's study skills for nurses.* London: Bailliere Tindall and RCN.

McGill, I and Beaty. L (1995) Continuing professional development. In I McGill and L Beaty (eds) *Action learning.* (2nd edn.) London: Kogan Page, pp198–208.

Mezirow, J (1981) A critical theory of adult learning and education. *Adult Education*, 32 (1), 3–24.

Moon, J (1999a) *Learning journals: A handbook for academics, students and professional development.* London: Kogan Page.

Moon, J (1999b) *Reflection in learning and professional development: Theory and practice.* London: Kogan Page.

Mumm, AM (1997) Teaching critical thinking in social work practice courses. *Journal of Social Work Education*, 33 (1), 75–85.

Newman, T (2000) *Developing evidence based practice in social care: Locating, appraising and using research findings on effectiveness. Guidelines for practitioners.* Exeter: CEBSS.

Nixon, S and Murr, A (2006) Practice learning and the development of professional practice. *Social Work Education,* 25 (8), 798–811.

O'Reilly, D, Cunningham, L and Lester, S (eds) (1999) *Developing the capable practitioner.* London: Kogan Page.

O'Sullivan, T (1999) *Decision making in social work.* London: Macmillan.

Philips, V and Bond, C (2004) Undergraduates' experiences of critical thinking. *Higher Education Research and Development.* 23 (3), 276–94

Plath, D, English, B, Connors, L and Beveridge, A (1999) Evaluating the outcomes of intensive critical thinking instruction for social work students. *Social Work Education,* 18 (2), 207–17.

QAA (2001) *The framework for higher education qualifications in England, Wales and Northern Ireland.* Available from: www.qaa.ac.uk/academicinfrastructure/FHEQ/EWNI/default.asp#framework Accessed Jan 2005.

Race, P (2001) *The lecturers toolkit* (2nd edn) London: Kogan Page.

Rolfe, G, Freshwater, D and Jasper, M (2001) *Critical reflection for nursing and the helping professions. A user's guide.* London: Palgrave.

Saltiel, D (2003) Teaching reflective research and practice on a Post Qualifying Child Care programme. *Social Work Education,* 22 (1), 105–11.

Schön, D (1983) *The reflective practitioner: How professionals think in action.* London: Temple Smith.

Schön, D (1987) *Educating the reflective practitioner.* London: Temple Smith.

Secker, J (1993) *From theory to practice in social work. The development of social work students' practice.* Aldershot: Avebury.

Sheldon, B and Chilvers, R (2000) *Evidence-based social care. A study of prospects and problems.* Lyme Regis: Russell House.

Smith, F (1992) *To think; In language, learning and education*. London: Routledge.

Sotto, E (1994) *When teaching becomes learning: A theory and practice of teaching*. London: Continuum.

Stokoe, L (2003) *Critical analysis skills.* Worcester: University College Worcester. www.worc.ac.uk/departs/psycho/Teaching/Critical.html. Accessed 7 Jan 2004.

Taylor, CP and White, S (2001) Knowledge, truth and reflexivity: The problem of judgment in social work. *Journal of Social Work,* 1 (37), 37–59.

Van Manen, M (1995) On the epistemology of reflective practice. *Teachers and Teaching; Theory and Practice.* 1 (1), 33–50.

Watson, F, Burrows, H and Player, C (2002) *Integrating theory and practice in social work education*. London: Jessica Kingsley.

Weick, A, Rapp, C, Sullivan, WP and Kristhardt, W (1989) A strengths perspective for social work practice. *Social Work,* 34, 350–4.

Williams, S and Rutter, L (2007) *Enabling and assessing work-based learning for social work. Supporting the development of professional practice*. Birmingham: Learn to Care.

Yelloly, M and Henkel, M (eds) (1995) *Learning and teaching in social work: Towards reflective practice*. London: Jessica Kingsley.

Appendix
Harvard referencing

The following brief guidance is based on the system that Bournemouth University uses and our experience. Please refer to your own institution's regulations.

Bournemouth University, like many universities, uses the Harvard referencing system as advised in the following British Standards:

BS 5605:1990. *Recommendations for citing and referencing published material*, 2nd edn. BSI (Dorset House Library – 028.7 BRI)

BS 1629:1989. *Recommendations for references to published materials*. BSI. (Dorset and Bournemouth House Libraries – 028.7 BRI)

References are cited in two different places. Firstly, at the point at which a source is referred to in the text of the work; secondly, in a list at the end of the work – the reference list. The following examples are all fictitious and any resemblance to existing works is purely coincidental.

Citing in the text

The Harvard system is also called the author/date method because sources are referred to in the text by giving the author's surname and the year of publication. For citations referring to particular parts of the document, the page number may be given after the year.

Examples

(a) Smith (2005) showed us the importance of referencing in academic work…

(b) The five particular ways in which referencing affects academic work have been clearly explored by Smith (2005, pp24–5)…

(c) Referencing is very important in academic work (Smith, 2005)…

Tip: Many people find it difficult to remember where the brackets go. A simple tip is to consider whether the author's name forms part of the text. In our first two examples above, the name Smith forms part of the sentence, so it is not put in the brackets (only the date). In the third example, the name Smith does not form part of the sentence, thus the author's name goes in the brackets with the date (Smith, 2005).

Problem – no author?

• The author (i.e. the originator) may be the organisation shown most prominently in the source as responsible for the content in its published form should be given.

- For certain kinds of work, e.g. dictionaries or encyclopaedias, or if an item is the co-operative work of many individuals, none of whom have a dominant role, e.g. videos or films, the title may be used instead of an originator or author.
- For completely anonymous works, use 'Anon.' instead of a name.

Problem – no date?

- If an exact year or date is not known, an approximate date preceded by c may be given in square brackets , e.g. [c 1750].
- If you can't make an approximate date then you state 'no date' in square brackets, i.e. [no date].

Reference list

At the end of the work the references are listed in alphabetical order of originator's surnames.

NB: A bibliography is a list of all works that have influenced the writer of the text, not just the ones directly referred to. You will usually be asked for a reference list rather than a bibliography.

Problem – the same author is being listed more than once

- If you have cited more than one item by a specific author, they should be listed chrono-logically (earliest first), and by letter (2001a, 2001b) if the author has published more than one work in a specific year.

The elements of a reference need to be in a specific order. Here are just a few (fictitious) examples:

Books

Author/originator (surname and then initials),
Year of publication
Title
Edition (if not the first)
Place of publication
Publisher.

e.g.   Smith, B., 2005. *How to reference*. London: Bloggs Publishing.

Problem – the book chapter has a different author

- You make the chapter author the main originator and give the title of the chapter and its pages as well, as follows:

    JONES, J.R., 2005. Citation and plagiarism. In: B Smith (ed) *How to reference*. London: Bloggs Publishing, pp502–10.

Problem – the person you are referencing is being quoted in another work

- In the text you must cite both authors, e.g. as follows:

A study by Harris and Keeble (1996, cited in Smith, 2005, p24) showed that...

but only list the work you have used, i.e. Smith, in the reference list at the end of your work.

Journals

Author/originator (surname and then initials)
Year of publication
Title of article
Title of journal
Volume number and (part number)
Page numbers of contribution

e.g.   Smith, B., 2004. The referencing nightmare.
       Journal of Referencing and Citation, 9 (1), 28–41.

Websites

Author/originator (surname and then initials)
Year
Title.
Place of publication: Publisher (if ascertainable)
Available from: URL. Accessed Date.

e.g.   Smith Referencing Company (*c* 2003). *Referencing guidelines.* London: Smith Referencing Co. Available from: www.smithreferencing.co.uk. [Accessed 23 Oct 2004.]

Index

Learning Resources
Centre